Don De Pasquale
1819 Stuart St
Berkeley, CA 94703
841-1361

RESTRUCTURING
OUR
SCHOOLS

RESTRUCTURING
OUR
SCHOOLS
A Primer On Systemic Change

by W. Patrick Dolan

edited by
Lilot Moorman

Systems & Organization/Kansas City

The publisher offers discounts on this book when ordered in quantity for special sales. For more information please contact:

Systems & Organization
P. O. Box 7135
Kansas City, MO 64113-0135

Library of Congress Catalogog Card Number: 94-67028

Dolan, W. Patrick
       Restructuring Our Schools/W. Patrick Dolan

ISBN 0-9641690-0-2

To Geraldine Dolan --

In gratitude to a mother and teacher
of strength, conviction,
and Irish fire.

Contents

Appendices

Contents

PREFACE

This book arose out of a series of seminars that I offered across the country on site-based decision making from 1991 to 1994. They were sponsored by the American Association of School Administrators, the National Education Association, and the American Federation of Teachers, as well as the National Association of Elementary School Principals.

I began tentatively, using the fifteen years of private sector work with unions and management as a stalking horse.   But the message back was strong and continuous: "This is our journey too, and the stories could be from our school district, our community."

So, slowly I wove together the materials below out of our educational restructuring efforts in Wisconsin, Minnesota, Nebraska, North Carolina, and Washington state.

The principles are straightforward. There is a single system in place. It has certain characteristics. We must change some of them profoundly to offer quality through empowered teachers and learners. We cannot be afraid of the customer-parents, but must bring them "in" correctly. All else in the structure must be rearranged to support this.

Second, the entire system is *one*, and to change a school is to change a district, its union, board, and management. And eventually to change the state educational structures as well. Anything else will be short-lived and false.

But how to perform the restructuring with grace and skill -- that is the fun, the dance, the sojourn.

Over the last four or five years, I have offered the material included in this book in many configurations and to many audiences. One of the more interesting observations that comes after the seminar from various life experiences and positions within education and without is the following observation: "This whole thing has been very helpful to me in the following way -- What you have done is lay out a large map much of which I understand and some of which I have journeyed, but have very seldom seen all the boundaries."

Time and again they use the analogy of a map and their own experience as some sort of journey. Much of it has to do with the way I believe I constantly visualize the system and the parts, but the other is that I think understandings in systemic fashion really are understandings of organizational "maps," relationships of things to other things, parts to parts, pieces to pieces, and the attempt to establish true and unchanging moral and educational axes that do not move.

But I am also always taken by the amazing contradiction included in the metaphor of the journey and map. We make maps out of great desire for exactitude and knowledge of where we are and where we are going. They prevent us from getting "lost." And so on one hand what we want out of maps for our journey is assurance of carefulness, exactitude and low risk. It is to avoid misturns and mistakes. But a journey itself, particularly to new places, is made because of a sense of adventure, a desire for discovery, a push to something new. There is the desire for something not known, something that has appeared as desirable in our imagination and in our dreams.

That is always true as we redesign our lives and our organizations, and doubly true of our schools. We embark on the journey with great trepidation because of its importance. We do not want to make a mistake, and yet if the journey is to have any real quality or worth, it must be founded on dreams and risks and adventure. It must be a reach of a true learner and learning organization.

In that is the tension between map and adventure. The true sojourn.

W. Patrick Dolan
Kansas City, April, 1994

Chapter One: The Second Day of Creation

Go before a group of five hundred professional educators, and ask them: "In how many sincere, long-term attempts at change have you participated?" The average, you will hear, is five or six in a thirty year career. Then ask them: "How many have achieved deep, long-lasting results?" And they will *howl* with laughter. They're here to tell you: There is something unique about school systems that defies substantive change.

1

They are wrong. There is nothing unique about public education in its ability to resist change. Just look at the business pages of your newspaper on any given day. Then ask yourself, "How could this happen? How did Sears/Westinghouse/Pan Am/GM/IBM/Woolworth (pick your favorite Ozymandias) go wrong? These were untouchable organizations. What happened?"

For fifteen years I've been working in private industry, watching with fascination and sometimes bemusement as large organizations struggle with change. For the past few years I've been applying those lessons to public education, helping school systems grapple with many of the same issues. This book is about what it takes to change structures and the men and women who create them.

Like any good journey of the imagination, it begins with a metaphor - two metaphors in fact. Which one you choose will determine the path you take.

REPLACING PARTS

Imagine a car. It is not running properly. Old Bessie is not getting the mileage, she is not getting the acceleration, she sounds choked up even when it is not cold.

You take her to a mechanic. He replaces the catalytic converter. That is all it took; Bessie runs like a new car. It may be years before you have another problem.

Now imagine a school district. Something is wrong. Iowa Test of Basic Skills (ITBS) scores are dropping, teachers are leaving the district, and there are ominous rumblings from the parents.

You call in the experts. They identify the problem; they outline a series of solutions; the school board approves it. You spend three years and a considerable part of your discretionary budget implementing several parts of their recommendation.

> **"Organizational change becomes a visit to the `parts' store for the proper upgrade, and school improvement is a series of well-intentioned tweaking and new `bits.'"**

And, now, it is five years later. The teachers are on strike; three of the district schools are in the bottom tier of state rankings; and newspapers editorialize the virtues of a voucher system.

The underlying metaphor in both these stories is a "mechanism," a thing that is put together of parts. With a mechanism, if you can identify the piece that is faulty, needs replacement or upgrading, you can fix it.

Most efforts at organizational change are grounded in the mechanistic metaphor. If you follow it, your educational strategies will be piecemeal, part by part: inservice training here, new principal there, new curricular slice over yonder. Organizational change becomes a visit to the "parts" store for the proper upgrade, and school improvement is a series of well-intentioned tweaking and new "bits."

SEEING THE SYSTEM AS A WHOLE

There is, however, another frame you can use. If your metaphor is organic - that is to say it is closer to a living organism than to a machine - then everything changes. When you look at a school or school district from this perspective, you see a "whole" system with deeply interconnected sub-systems.

Any approach that sees the system as one overarching reality means that *if you touch any significant part, you touch it all. You couldn't conceive of changing the role of a group of teachers without a strategy for the principal, for other groups of teachers, for students, for parents, and so on.* It is all interconnected much the way a living system is.

A school system is not like a car. This seems so obvious. But the cultural bias that makes us think of it as a machine is so powerful, and the temptation to find the right part to fix it is so compelling, that we fall for it. The mechanistic model promises what everyone wants - a quick, clean, measurable solution to an identified problem - and all of it with a minimum of disruption. No wonder it is a seductive model, and no wonder we keep working it in the hope that if only we could find the right mechanic, and if only she could obtain the necessary parts, we would be back on the road to quality education.

But even if we were too smart to fall into the mechanistic trap, even if we chose the organic metaphor and rejected piecemeal solutions, even if we had learned from our mistakes...even then, we'd have a problem.

THE SYSTEM IN PLACE

If I were writing in German, I would be able to invent a new word to describe this phenomenon. I would call it the System-In-Place-Over-Against-Which-You-Start. That is no small presenting problem.

On the first day of creation God walked out and could do anything at all. On the second day, She walked out again, this time with a bunch of stars in her pocket. But now She would have to hang them *over against* what She did the first day. There is something already there. From the second day of creation on, the system-in-place has been the fundamental issue that conditions every change. No one since has gotten to invent an organizational change from scratch. There is always something over which you are going to restructure.

If you pretend that it is not there, or naively believe you can paint over it, some months or years later you will find the old picture staring back at you, scarcely altered. Perhaps a line or two shaded, a color darkened, but unmistakenly, triumphantly the earlier canvas.

What's more, the system-in-place will actively *resist* change - and with a certain ferocity to boot. There is a fundamental, relational, and intellectual consistency in every system that translates into a powerful drive to retain its equilibrium. It is in a "Steady State," and needs to stay put.

DISAPPEARING PILOT PROJECTS

There is an awful fascination in watching the Steady State at work. You can see it in the phenomenon of the "pilot project." Take the example of a school district, in which someone has a bright idea for doing things differently. Let's say the district says, "Okay, we don't know if it works or not, but let's do a pilot project."

"As long as the pilot makes no difference..., the system leaves it alone. But as soon as the small pilot starts to change things significantly, the larger system ... quickly, with a force you cannot imagine, reaches out and pulls that little experiment back to itself."

The theory is that the larger system will sit off to one side, watch the pilot project, and if it works, say "Wonderful, it works. Let's move to it."

That is the theory. In practice, exactly the opposite happens. As long as the pilot makes no difference at all, the home system leaves it alone. But as soon as the small pilot starts to change things significantly, the larger system takes a good hard look. And then quickly, with a force you cannot imagine, it reaches out and pulls that little experiment back to itself. Sometime later, it is as though nothing ever happened.

The educational landscape is littered with the bones of wonderful pilot projects, really successful little experiments that lasted for four or five years and then, somehow, died. You can picture educators sitting around campfires, old women and old men, stirring ashes and swapping stories of those heroic adventures, and wondering what happened. They never knew what hit them.

TO KNOW SOMETHING
IS NOT TO BE ABLE TO DO IT

Right now in the United States, we are observing a truly dramatic illustration of the power of the Steady State. General Motors and the United Auto Workers (UAW) - two very large systems - have struggled for years to reinvent their relationship. Eight years ago, in the face of all their old pathology, they went to Tennessee and built a plant together. They created one of the best car plants in the United States, with the best union-management relations in the country based on a four-page contract full of high-trust language, of "We'll do it together." And within a few years, together, they were building some of the highest quality cars in the country. Walk through the plant and you'll see people full of energy, helping each other, proud of what they do and caring a lot about what happens to their company. Talk to clients, more of the same.

Now, in theory, Chevrolet, Buick, Pontiac and GMC would be sitting there watching this little exercise and saying, "Oh ho, that's how to do it," And after a few months of soul-searching they'd start doing things the Saturn way. Instead we are seeing something else.

Saturns are selling like hotcakes. General Motors needs those sales and they're in a hurry for Saturn to make more. So, the company is starting to lean on the division for more cars. They've gone to two shifts, and maybe they'll go to three. They've added one on Sunday. General Motors has raised the bar to demand profitability within three years of start-up - an unheard of achievement. In the process, they are creating enormous strains on the relationship with the UAW, and real concerns about whether they will be able to maintain the quality of the product.

Rather than General Motors reinventing itself, what we seem to be seeing is the larger system, with all its power, pulling that pilot back.

This is not an indictment of General Motors, or the good will of the people involved. The power of the Steady State to resist change is well documented. You don't even need to go through the literature. Just think about people who have been talking about changing their lives, or some behavior for years, or those men and women you see wandering through airports reading self-help books. They have all these wonderful ideas, but somehow nothing ever changes.

"...you need a second strategy, a strategy for unsticking the Steady State already in place."

CONTENT AND PROCESS: A SECOND STRATEGY

The point is you do need "content" strategies - ideas about new behavior - new ways to teach children, to arrange material, to create new learning environments. And at the same time you need a *second* strategy, a strategy for unsticking the Steady State already in place. Site-based decision making is this type of strategy. It is without content. But it is a powerful "process" strategy to create torque on all parts of the system as you begin to implement good ideas about how to teach children better. If you do not take into account the present system in place, and try to move only with content ideas, the System-In-Place will snap you back, and you will join those other folks sitting around the campfire swapping tales.

Second, knowledge is only half an answer. Wonderful new educational ideas are not enough. To know something is not to be able to do it. There must be a process strategy as well to take on the "stuckness" of the present system. In this little book, we are about this second strategy.

Any hope of changing educational systems in any fundamental sense is conditioned on an understanding of the system in place. There are certain consistent principles that should shape a strategy for a change process, certain givens that provide a starting point.

Principles of a Change Process

1. A preexisting social structure is always in place when you begin.

2. All of a system's parts are organically interconnected with one another.

3. The system will resist change in fundamental and powerful ways.

4.   The system in place in each organization is quite unique. You must pay careful attention to its characteristics, its particular history, its evolving relationships and the leadership patterns that have made it what it is today.

5.   Unique as the particular system is, it shares certain fundamental attributes with almost every other organizational system in the Western world. Understanding those generic characteristics is a good place to begin.

The first critical decision in school reform is to determine where the system is. It is not a segment such as schedule or curriculum. It is not an individual school. It is not even an individual district. The "system" in the United States, is the state. We have fifty quite distinct systems, as a matter of fact. The question really is, "Where does the thing I am trying to move, begin and end? Where does it cease being held in place by other parts?" That is where the system begins.

Chapter Two: The Structure of the Western Organizational Model

We know something about the system-in-place. All over the Western world, in Europe or the United States or Latin America or even Eastern Europe - when you walk up to any given organization, you are looking at something basically similar to every other organization. There may be regional, cultural, or occupational variations, but basically it is the same model.

11

It is a variation of an old military model - a Roman model. It derives from the two fundamental organizational experiences in the history of Western culture. One was military and the other ecclesiastical.

Wherever the Romans sent their armies, they left behind infrastructures, and those infrastructures lasted for more than a thousand years, imprinting all other institutions of society. They were based on a fundamentally military approach that centered power, authority, and decision making at the top of a descending pyramid of command-demand.

We are so accustomed to this pyramid that we take the structure for granted. In fact, other cultures in other parts of the world have found, at different times, different ways of organizing large groups of people around complex tasks. But this Roman military model has so permeated our own culture that we can generalize some amazingly consistent attributes that hold, whether it is a large industrial complex or a small rural school district.

The fundamental characteristic of this model is that power and authority for the direction of the enterprise are centered at the top of the pyramid. The military command orientation has powerful ramifications on decision making and information flow. Most strategic thinking is done at the top of the pyramid. The generals sit on higher ground at some place removed from the din of battle, observe the big picture and develop strategy.

The middle tier of the pyramid is closer to the engagement. It is allowed tactical interpretation of pieces of the strategy. Somewhere down in the valley, this or that squadron leader decides where it is safe to cross the river, and which groups to send first.

Finally, at the bottom two or three levels of the pyramid, the grunts live, work, fight, and die. There is little or no decision-making role for those who carry the spears. Their job is to do what they're told and not to ask questions.

Access to information follows the decision-making pattern. There is a clear correlation between where you are in the hierarchy and how much you know. Those at the strategic level should have almost all the

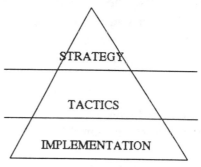

Figure 1. Traditional Military Model

information with respect to an undertaking. Down on the tactical level, there should be at least enough information to make sense of a particular piece of responsibility.

By the time you get to the level of implementation, there is little need to know much about the activity. In fact, there are sound military reasons to keep the spear-carriers in the dark. The only place where you are actually exposed to the enemy is at the bottom of the pyramid, so it makes all kinds of sense to restrict their access to information.

Thus, it is very important where you find yourself in the pyramid. In this top-down, command-demand structure you are reminded every day where you belong in the hierarchy. Your rank tells the world how much you need to know, and how much say you have about it.

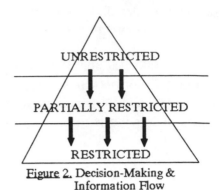

Figure 2. Decision-Making & Information Flow

"...it is very important where you find yourself in the pyramid."

Certainly, there were sound military reasons behind this information/decision-making prejudice in the military model. But, curiously, it was passed down intact to modern times and to the most benign undertakings. Today this stratification of decision-making and information access holds true whether you are looking at a thirty-employee construction crew or a huge multinational corporation employing thousands and thousands of people: It is going to be top-down, with heavy emphasis on control, clearly stratified, and with restricted access to information.

This military model endures for several centuries and then makes an interesting marriage. Toward the end of the Roman Empire it joins with the emerging ecclesiastical structure. The Roman Empire becomes the Holy Roman

Empire, and Christianity becomes the Roman Catholic Church. Now there is a further dimension to the authority of the organization, for somehow the decisions of this human organization are linked to the Divine. In fact, in several critical areas when this organization speaks, by definition, God speaks. This lends an incredible authority to its hierarchy. And, for the next ten centuries, this ecclesiastical/military/civil organization carried and deepened the model throughout the Western world, down through the middle ages and up to the Renaissance and the Protestant Reformation. Somehow, even today, we have invested our organizational structures with that same authority and that same power.

THE MILITARY MODEL
MEETS THE SCIENTIFIC REVOLUTION

For fifteen hundred years this model remains essentially unchanged. Then, with the start of the Sixteenth Century and the beginnings of the Scientific Revolution, a new paradigm is superimposed on this Roman/ecclesiastical model. Scientific disciplines emerge; the Renaissance man gives way to the specialist.

The known world becomes more complex and diverse; new methodologies and languages emerge. It becomes necessary to deal with both information and tasks by dividing them into smaller, more manageable units. By the time you get to the middle of the nineteenth century and the Industrial Revolution, this organizational experience is already deeply rooted and in place, ready to become the factory model. Large groups of people are being gathered together around increasingly complex tasks.   Now, a new element is added to the traditional military ecclesiastical model. Span of control and division into smaller

**"In fact, courses are usually taught
as if they have no relationship to each other."**

organizational units emerge as features of the factory structure and within the larger organization, the emerging orthodoxy is that the entire structure should be organized along lines of specialization. We have finally come to the deeply gridded, vertically and horizontally divided pyramid that characterizes the modern organizational experience.

By the beginning of the Twentieth Century this Western organizational model exists in every sphere of life. The typical industrial enterprise resembles a cluster of silos, each sheltering its own little world: Finance, Human Resources, Engineering, Production, Purchasing and so on. The configuration in a service organization or a governmental body may have some different disciplines, but has essentially the same look to it.

Walk through the command and control center of any large school district (it's usually known as "Downtown" and it is often housed in an enormous structure that has obviously been built to last) and you will experience this phenomenon. You will walk through a long hall, with signs directing you to the different disciplines, housed in separate offices. You will climb the stairs to a second floor laid out along similar silos of specialization, with slightly larger offices. And finally you will reach a top floor that houses the apex of the pyramid in large offices labeled "Superintendent," "Deputy Superintendent," "Director of Curriculum Development" and so on.   It's the organizational pyramid cast in concrete and paneled in wood.

Interestingly, this probably isn't very different than the public high school ten blocks away. A sixteen year old girl's daily experience is to walk through a series of cognitive silos -six of them, fifty minutes long - every day. It is her problem to put them together.   In fact, courses are usually taught as if they have no relationship to each other.

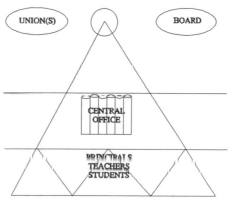

Figure 3.   Layers & Silos in Educational System

The phenomenon is the same throughout the Western world. Wherever you encounter the Steady State, this is what you will find: a top down, strongly authoritarian, tight control of information, deeply layered pyramid, gridded into vertical and horizontal silos.

That is what it looks like.   Now, how does it behave?

Chapter Three:
Numbers and
Ciphers

As the specializations grew, and the diversity and complexity of their languages and methodologies increased, so did the difficulties of integration and communication between areas of specialization. By the 1920s and 1930s the emerging solution was a special language for communication among the silos and up through the hierarchy. That language was quantitative and analytical. It allowed the general management to ask similar questions of each of the diverse activities, and get answers in a common language that facilitated comparison, measurement and control. One of the more amazing examples of this use of numbers in its starkest iteration was during the Vietnam conflict.

For thousands of years military success or progress had been measured in terms of territory gained. It soon became clear in Vietnam that that yardstick was basically useless: you could take the same piece of jungle over and over again and the enemy would turn up behind you, among you, and in the place you had just taken yesterday. Faced with this dilemma the Western command attempted to find a short form for understanding what was being accomplished. The emerging language of this command in Vietnam was body count and kill ratios. It was a dramatic example of a culture trusting that numbers alone could tell the story.

"The numbers, even when they are understood to be only part of the total reality, are left on the table at the end of a discussion as the single and almost complete description of the endeavor."

Alfred North Whitehead had a very powerful description of the use of purely quantitative terms. He called it the "fallacy of misplaced concreteness." By that I think he simply meant that the half-life of quantitative language is much longer than most other descriptors. The numbers, even when they are understood to be only part of the total reality, are left on the table at the end of a discussion as the single and almost complete description of the endeavor.

It's as though you took the complexity of educating twenty-five third-graders in different communities around the country, with their diversity of backgrounds, interactions, the work itself and its progress, and tried to describe the results of this enormously intricate and complex set of interactions through the simple language of individual test scores by classroom, school and district.

The danger, of course, is that those test scores would tend to become not only a shorthand for <u>some</u> dimension of the activity, but *the single descriptor of what was being achieved,* and the single goal of the organization. If you begin to believe that this is the whole reality or even a substantial part of it, then tactics and strategies will follow, probably to some lovely educational Vietnam. The numbers may be true. But they are not the truth.

As if that weren't enough, we have compounded the problem by adding a temporal kick. Whatever occurs within this top-down, quite layered, authoritarian, vertically and horizontally gridded organizational approach that uses numbers as its language, is expected to happen in some fairly fast sequence. No matter how great the complexity, or how difficult the endeavor, *some quick results are required. So, the language of this orthodoxy is not only quantitative, but quantitative short-term* and the result is that there is a deep prejudice toward short-term and quantitative endeavors over long-term and highly qualitative goals.

MOTIVATION FOR THE LONG HAUL

"To keep people truly motivated over the long-term you must look at the intrinsic motivators."

The final piece of this complex human system is the question of motivation. The problem of how to keep the troops with you over the long haul has always been present, at least since Xenophon, and by the mid-twentieth century we began to know a good deal about it.

Some thirty-five years ago Frederick Herzberg, one of the most respected researchers in work motivation, outlined a set of fundamental distinctions that have always been present from the time that human beings began to organize themselves. He made the distinction between motivators that lie *within* a human being, which he called *intrinsic,* and motivators that are *outside* the man or woman, or *extrinsic* to them.

Extrinsic issues are such things as pay, benefits, working conditions and the way you are managed or treated by your organization or supervision - in other words, all the traditional carrots we provide. These are external to the individual, and they are enormously demotivating if they are "off" with respect to judgments of fairness and equity.

But - and this was one of the most important distinctions Herzberg made - *when things finally are equal, just, and in balance, they are incapable of becoming long-term motivators.* To make them fair and equitable simply does no more than to take away their demotivating power.

To keep people truly motivated over the long-term, according to Herzberg, you must look at the *intrinsic* motivators. These are the things that originate inside a person and that make a difference in their caring and individual effort. There are various lists, but Herzberg provides as interesting a catalogue as any. They are:

1.   *Information,* so that people understand what it is they are being asked to do, and how it fits into a series of larger units, such as a school, a school district, or a state strategy for education of children.

2.   A modicum of *control* over their work, particularly
        as it relates to information about goals and
        measurements, and the individuals' direct delivery
        towards those goals.

3.   *Respect*, for them as individuals, for who they are
        and what they do. This probably is linked deeply to
        the first two motivators, information and control.

4.   Finally, in Herzberg's language, the *chance to grow*,
        as a human being. Herzberg did not mean it to be
        a shorthand form for movement up the hierarchy,
        but rather the chance to grow according to one's
        spirit and one's own pace, as a human being in
        one's work.

Source: Herzberg, F. 1987. "One more time: How do you motivate employees?"
           Harvard Business Review. Boston, MA. (September/October 1987)

           Frederick Herzberg, Distinguished Professor of Management at the University
           of Utah, was head of the department of psychology at Case Western Reserve
           University when he wrote this article. His writings include the book *Work and
           the Nature of Man (World, 1966).*

The tragedy of this description of motivators and
demotivators is that, by definition, the orthodoxy of our
Western model denies those persons at the bottom of the
pyramid any chance at the intrinsic motivators. They exist
in a state of no information, no power, very little respect
and a feeling of being trapped forever in this impotency and
disenfranchisement.

MOTIVATORS

EXTRINSIC	INTRINSIC
Pay	Information
Benefits	Control Over Work
Working Conditions	Respect
Supervision	Chance To Grow

And when you need these people - when you are in competition, say with the Japanese, and quality improvement and ongoing problem-solving become life or death issues - then you find that these people have "gone to ground." When you need the people who do the work to deliver the quality, *they are not there.*

ANGRY WORKERS IN THE TRENCHES

Early-on in my career I had one of those moments that suddenly illuminate things. I was interviewing an hourly worker as part of a diagnostic for a client in Waterloo, Iowa. After about three hours, he turned to me and said, "Listen, you want to know what it's like? Here it is. I'm fifty-five years old. I have a seventh-grade education. I know how to bend metal, that's all I know how to do. I've worked here for twenty-eight years. I've put three kids through college. I make $50,000 a year. I know I could never make that kind of money anywhere else. AND I HATE THIS PLACE!"

He said it with such passion it took my breath away. I looked at him; he looked at me, and went on, "When I walked in here that first day twenty-eight years ago, and for every day since then for twenty-eight years this place has said to me: You are stupid. You don't care. And you can't be trusted. And, *I hate it.*"

This is the rage at the bottom of the pyramid. And because they can't live day in and day out with this rage, they hunker down and get safe. Somehow the rage flows under, but the result is that you are left with a workforce that is not only not with you, but against you.

At the deepest levels of our organizations, the men and women who do the implementation are uninformed, unempowered, disenfranchised, and seriously alienated from the work of the larger organization and even sometimes from their own particular work entity. It is a tough profile, a sad one, but difficult to deny.

AND WHAT ABOUT THE SCHOOLS?

The private sector has no particular lock on this model. When we turn to public education, the structures, although unique, bear powerful resemblances to this orthodoxy. Granted, America is one of the few major industrial nations that does not set educational policy at the national level, nor attempt to monitor, control and measure it from there . . . at least not yet.

"...a cursory glance would tell us that that adult's environment is those children's environment. They are one and the same, and if one is alienated and controlled, so will the other be."

The states and local school districts traditionally have been the source of direction for educational policy and goals. But, in recent years, combinations of federal law and state directives have come together increasingly to create bureaucratic requirements and reporting layers. At the bottom of the pyramid is a typical rural, suburban, or urban classroom with 25 children and their teacher. If other people set the goals, draw up the indicators, and then announce that they will monitor and assess to make sure work is done at acceptable quality levels, they are, in effect, saying, "You can't be trusted." The question is whether the tone, the feeling, and the ultimate experience is any different in that classroom than it is for a steelworker or an auto worker.

And the question we will examine later, is if a message of mistrust is given to that teacher day in and day out, what type of learning environment will emerge? There is a strange disconnect for many educational reformers who say, "Let's talk about what's good for kids. I don't have time to play games with these adults." But a cursory glance would tell us that that adult's environment is those children's environment. They are one and the same, and if one is alienated and controlled, so will the other be.

Teaching and learning is the work of schools. Those activities occur in the same space and time and are as deeply connected as any transaction could be. High control approaches to instruction, punitive contexts of assessment, competitive learning environments, all will produce an identical alienation in children. The "learner" would then begin to distance herself from the enterprise in much the same way adults do.

Chapter Four: The Fundamental Dysfunctions

The first look at this Western orthodoxy in operation reveals a supremely efficient, rationally organized structure, perfectly adapted to carrying out large, complex tasks. In fact, when you consider a logistical triumph like Operation Desert Storm, you can see the genius of the model. A closer look reveals something else.

The model is based on getting an answer on strategy "right" at the top and arranging all other components to hold it steady and carry it out. But, it is inflexible, once frozen, and only succeeds if the time sequence is short or movement and change "outside" are glacial. If the world of needs and customers begins to speed up and change rapidly, the model is in great trouble.

The problems first began to surface widely after World War II, and a pattern slowly emerged. These were no mere glitches. They were fundamental weaknesses, deeply ingrained in the organizational model itself. What's more, no one seemed to have a corner on them; public or private, industrial or service, the failures of the model were generic.

They remain generic today, and schools share the malaise with most of our other structures.

In general, the problems center around four major dysfunctions:

1.   *Information Flow.* This is a non-listening system that can neither retrieve its own data, nor learn from it. It's a command model, not a consultative one.

2.   *The Un-Team.* It is a non-integrated structure in which groups work in silos of specialization, and individuals compete with one another for power, position, and resources.

3.   *The Short-Term Quantitative Bias.* The system is driven by short-term quantitative measurements that lead to dangerous misinterpretation of the situation.

4.   *The Morale of the Troops.* It cannot sustain the energy, talent and commitment of those who do the work.

INFORMATION FLOW: WHAT'S GOING ON?

There are two requirements for managing successfully within this model. First, you must be able to give clear kinds of commands and directions. Second, you must be able to understand the results of the strategy, and change course and direction as needed. This means the system must send information up from the level of implementation in an open and constant fashion. This ability to listen is vital to a quick-response, flexible organization.

"The system must send information up from the level of implementation in an open and constant fashion."

If you want a picture of what happens to non-listening systems, look at what happened to Sears Roebuck. Back in the 1950s, it dominated the rural market with its catalog sales. Then a funny, little, unknown company in Arkansas, started to build stores on country crossroads near the towns where Sears customers lived. The stores were called Wal-Mart and they were hiring employees who knew everyone in the county, to stand in the doorway and greet people as they came in. And Sears started to lose market share - more and more - year after year. But its management kept right on sending out catalogues and waiting for the customers to come back. How could they not know something was going on? It didn't happen over night.

It's very likely they really didn't know. People at the top of giant, bureaucratic organizations like Sears are isolated; they often don't have a clue. They're surrounded by a palace guard whose function is to buffer them from the outside world.

Sometimes those at the top are isolated by their own choice. The new chairman of Ford Motor Company admitted he did not own a car, had never had the experience of buying one from an American dealer, had never had the pleasure of taking one in for service, or struggle with having a warranty honored. In fact, he told a reporter for *The New York Times*, "I have never bought a car in America, and I don't see why I should do that. I know a lot of dealers, and I don't see why I have to buy a car to get in touch with the dealer-customer relationship."

To manage successfully, you simply must have people at the point of delivery who will tell you when something isn't working. It turns out that the Western model doesn't do that very well. In fact,

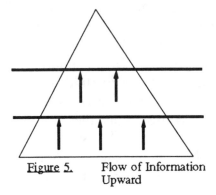

Figure 5.   Flow of Information Upward

Western organizational culture supports exactly the opposite behavior. It's enormously risky to move tough data up the hierarchy, especially in a blaming environment. This was not built to be a consultative, bottom-up model, and over the years it has become less and less so. Bureaucratic layers increase, and each layer tends to filter out what it considers unnecessary or troubling data as it moves up the organization.

The rare chief executive who truly wants to know what's going on at the point of delivery soon learns they can't break through. The general atmosphere of blame and fear that grows up over the years in our organizations discourages the passage of unadulterated data up through the organization, especially if there are undertones of failure. Heads roll when things go wrong, and no one wants to be associated with bad news. So, good data gets multiplied many times as it begins its way up, and bad data is played down or covered up. Ultimately, it means that those on the strategic decision-making level can't learn about themselves and their performance. They are operating in the dark, sometimes practically blind.

When I was first starting out as a young consultant fresh out of Harvard with my doctorate, I didn't have much to sell. So I'd walk into a corporate headquarters in Chicago or Cleveland and I'd say, "How are things going in Muncie?" And the CEO would say, "Beats me. I've got this stack of reports here but they don't tell me anything. I wish I knew." And I'd say, "Well, maybe I can help you."

So, I'd go down to Muncie and spend a week listening to the activity four or five layers down in the organization, and then I'd come back and say, "Here's what's going on in Muncie." A lot of people still make a good living doing that sort of thing. It's not a very good sign.

THE UN-TEAM

If we deliberately set out to create a model deeply antithetical to team work, we could not have done a better job than this Western orthodoxy. Its bureaucratization and specialization, and its emphasis on moving up the hierarchy has led to some deep behavioral consequences over the years. We have, in fact, created the un-team.

Characteristics of the Un-Team

1.   There is a *deeply competitive culture* that pits one group against another, hoping that out of this will come an overall driving organization.

2.   *"Language barriers"* between the specialized functions create an early warning of the difficulties of cross-silo or cross-function communication.

3.   The *fear of blame*, or being exposed in a mistake curtails the open sharing of information across the silos.

The problem, of course, is not that there is no team. There are teams, and they are quite clear. But they are the areas of specialization.

This is how it works: A woman has just graduated with her MBA, and she has taken a job as the first woman controller in a transmission plant in Lima, Ohio. Under the traditional Western model, she is about to make the mistake of her life.

Her mistake is that she plans to work as though her team at that transmission plant is made up of her peers who head the other departments: Engineering, Quality, Operations, etc. She hasn't caught on to the fact that *her* team in this model is supposed to be the Finance Department. That's who writes her ticket up and out of Lima. And those folks in Finance over at headquarters are saying "What kind of controller do we have in Lima? Does she understand what we are doing? Is she playing the game?"

If she starts lining up with the wrong team, they will say, "Hmm. Guess she doesn't understand that she is one of us. Too bad." And she'll die, still in Lima, at the age of 63.

The problem for the organization is that at every level of delivery, cross-functional, horizontal integration is of enormous importance. Somehow, the specializations *must* come together at the level of implementation, at tactical, and at strategic levels. Yet they don't. For the last thirty years organizations have been struggling to build some fabric of integration and team experience across these unintegrated and competitive silos. We have spent millions of dollars in the United States floating rivers and climbing trees...to build teams. Why are we having to do that?

And what about that woman stuck there in Lima and trying to figure it out? If she finally wises up and joins the right team, will that make her a team player? Not a chance. She didn't get her MBA by grinding away for the common good. If she is like most bright kids, somewhere around third-grade she looked to her right and looked to her left and thought to herself, "Well, someone is going to get

As, and the race is to the swift." And off she went.   Early-
on in her school experience, she began getting her
preparation for life.

**"...by the end of the year I'm going to look like a genius compared
to the others.   Why should I give away my breakthrough to the
rest of these guys?"**

SHARING INFORMATION WITH THE UN-TEAM

Not long ago I was sitting in a room with the vice-
president of operations of a major industrial company, and
his twelve plant managers. They were working on a quality
problem they're having with a big, expensive new piece of
machinery. They weren't doing well on that issue. As they
were struggling with the problem, one plant manager, the
one from Virginia, was sitting in the corner, biting his lip,
getting red-faced and not saying a word.

Finally, I interrupted them and said, "Jim, is
something wrong?" There was a long silence. Jim looked
up and slowly said, "Five months ago we had a
breakthrough and figured this problem out. We made these
kinds of adjustments, and figured out how to control that,
and we haven't had a problem since."

His boss literally came out of his chair screaming,
"Why haven't you told anyone?" And Jim, who is a
courageous and honest individual, looked him in the eye
and said, "Hey. I get evaluated against all the other plant
managers. The most important measure here is quality. If

things keep going the way they are, by the end of the year I'm going to look like a genius compared to the others. Why should I give away <u>my</u> breakthrough to the rest of these guys?"

Why should he? He would have to be the stupidest man in the world to do it. There is no reward in it. His "team" is really his competition, it's set up that way. School against school, student against student, district against district.

We tend to confine our view of competitiveness to the world of private sector corporations. However, from the beginnings of the U.S. educational system, the stress on individual competitiveness, learning environments of forced grading and grade distribution, and the general distrust of team learning and group problem-solving offers clues to the depth of this orthodoxy and its pervasiveness in education.

In the public sector and in the private sector, rewards for working in deep horizontal teams are scarce. As a matter of fact, very often people do so at great personal jeopardy to their long-term future in an organization, for it often puts you at odds with the special teams and your functional hierarchy.

SHORT TERM QUANTITY VERSUS LONG TERM QUALITY

Organizations have priorities, and usually the priority of the high command is felt in the field with stunning immediacy. The grunt understood the body count and kill ratio language of Vietnam very well. And, generally, he managed to satisfy that measure of performance.

Of course, there is nothing wrong with short-term quantitative results, nor are they necessarily antithetical to long-term qualitative results. Some of the best organizations in the world understand that balance and practice it daily. The trouble is, not many of them are in the United States.

I have a friend who manages a Toyota plant in this country. He came up by way of one of the American Big Three car companies. Shortly after he took the job with Toyota, I asked him, "Gary, what's the difference here?" And he answered, "It's simple. They only ask me two basic questions: 'Where are your quality indicators?' and 'What is your strategy for getting better?' They believe if we answer those questions, other measures will take care of themselves."

"We continue to define quality education by immediate improvement in test scores. If that should happen, then all the concern over quality would disappear overnight."

The problem with our model is that it is still largely driven by the quantitative short-term approach. The torque toward short-term numbers is so deeply embedded in our society that we can't even recognize when it distorts our long-term qualitative efforts.

When the first clarion call comes, or even the second or the third, to improve the quality of education in this country, the immediate demand comes for short-term, numerical data, to prove that the quality has changed. We continue to define quality education by immediate improvement in test scores. If that should happen, then all the concern over quality would disappear overnight.

The real danger is that, as in Vietnam, when things get complicated and hard to get hold of, the overwhelming tendency is to find a quantitative shorthand and try to drive it as fast and as hard as you can. And the thing to keep in mind through all of this is that *all the numbers around body counts and kill ratios were absolutely in our favor until the last helicopter out of Saigon.*

MORALE OF THE TROOPS

Where are those who do the work and fight the fight? What about the men and women who deliver the product and do the work at the base of the classic pyramid? They are, of course, the only people who touch the customer and do the "real" work of the organization. Everyone else in the organization has a role only insofar as it helps facilitate or support these men and women and girls and boys and that work.

Ordinarily, these people come to the enterprise with good will and openness, but they have two early experiences. First, they tend to make some mistakes early-on, because they're not yet skilled in the organization's work, nor its norms. Second, they see things that don't seem to make any sense and they naively ask questions.

If a young teacher had just entered the classroom to teach for the first time at the age of twenty-four, he might observe that he has encountered a group of children who appear to be neglected, angry, bored, and increasingly at odds with the school and its work.

If he carries this observation up the hierarchy to his immediate supervisor (notice, I have defined the circumstances to indicate he is bringing unsolicited negative data up the chain of command) he will be told, gently or not, to mind his own business, and get back to the classroom.

If he continues to see the same issue and feels that something should be done about it, perhaps he will move around his immediate supervisor to the next level of hierarchy. Now he has violated the chain of command as well. He's probably marked as insubordinate. Clearly, he is not off to a happy start in his career.

He'll probably get a quick lesson in organizational protocol. People do learn, and fairly rapidly, that this kind of unsolicited, bottom-up questioning is not part of their role.

Experiences like this have enormously powerful and negative results on the men and women in the ranks. In no time at all, they get the message they are supposed to get: they have very little right to know, or to question, and, increasingly, very little control over their own work. As a matter of fact, there are layers and layers of folks monitoring and evaluating their day-to-day activity. Within a year or two, that bright, idealistic, enthusiastic twenty-four-year-old will be well on his way to becoming a timeserver - unempowered, disenchanted, and alienated from the organization and its work. We don't intend that to happen. But the system, the culture, our entire orthodoxy drive the best people to ground, and we lose much of their creativity, caring, and power to make things better.

Every organization has some variation on these four vulnerabilities. I have not had a client in 15 years of working in the private sector who has not been grappling with some combination or other of these issues. Each institution feels the pain differently, but the model is powerful and pervasive enough to lead invariably to some combination of lack of team work, lack of a learning model, lack of long-term quality, and at the heart of it, the growing distance of the men and women who do the work from the organization itself and its goals.

In many of our schools, for many of the same reasons, this set of dysfunctions translates to our children. The work of learning, and their ownership of it, passes to others with much of the alienation and anger that follows.

Chapter Five: "Doctor, Heal Thyself."

In the early 1970s, entire industries in the United States -electronics, machine tools, steel - began slipping off the screen, one after another. People began to sit up and take notice. Slowly a realization grew that all was not right, and the problem might not be confined to just a specific company or industry. The middle management was incorrectly positioned, we were measuring the wrong things, and we were alienating the customer. But at the core, it began to dawn on managers that the hourly worker was not with the organization. As a matter of fact, there was growing data that he/she was disenfranchised from the organization, did not care about quality, and in some extreme cases might even be involved actively or passively in sabotage.

A senior executive in one of our largest corporations likes to tell the story of his early experience as an assembly line worker at a Studebaker plant while he was in college. As he tells it, "It was a rotten job, so we decided to get even. The two-door model that year had a spring-action handle hanging from the door frame so that rear-seat passengers could exit more easily. We figured out how to install it backwards so that it was absolutely impossible to use. You had to *crawl* out of the cars I worked on. It was the only satisfaction I got out of that job."

Studebaker went out of business. Other companies began looking for solutions. Some tried shutting down Rust Belt operations and moving to rural "green field" locations where they hoped workers would have "better attitudes." General Motors built such a facility on farmland near Lordstown, Ohio. Within a few years, Lordstown had the same problems as Detroit.

Other companies reacted angrily, blaming the unions, or even the customers who were abandoning them. Executives at Pan American World Airways actually wondered whether their problems were being caused by "the wrong sort of traveler." But some companies did begin to tinker with the model, usually in ways that only highlighted the problems.

"The first response was fear, anger, denial, and ferocious resistance, especially at the top."

PAYING ATTENTION TOO LATE

The experience of Ford Motor Company in the middle to late 1970s, is a powerful example of the struggling efforts at reform. Prior to this moment in its history, the Ford profile had been fairly consistent, if not pretty. It had a poor history of labor relations with the United Auto Workers (UAW). Its top management had been a hard-driving, series of flamboyant egos, constantly in conflict with the powerful and capricious Ford family itself. Product quality had been mediocre for years, but until the mid-1970s, Ford was still a viable presence in the automotive field. "Good enough for the little guy" was perhaps the best way to describe its organization and product. Then the disasters began; a combination of huge economic losses, a growing scandal based on unsafe designs, cover-ups, trials, Ralph Nader's public attacks, and the inevitable and growing damage in the marketplace.

Recent biographies and other chronicles give the impression that Ford leadership saw the issues of Japanese competition, customer dissatisfaction, and worker alienation, and thoughtfully began to craft its remarkable turnaround.
Not exactly. The first response was fear, anger, denial, and ferocious resistance, *especially at the top.* To forget this is to miss the first third of the story. It took a lot more pain before Ford finally found its way.

The point of this example is to call attention to the simple fact that, when the crisis occurs, it occurs with all the elements of the Western organizational orthodoxy still in place. And when a system is dysfunctional in fundamental ways, its early attempts at self-correction will generally be a magnification of its pathology. If this is true, what can we predict about the early attempts to reform?

Well, in the punitive, top-down command model, when the organization is in trouble, it doesn't occur to anyone early-on that the "commanders" have made a mistake. The first response is that the "soldiers" have not fought well. As Rosabeth Moss Kantor so succinctly puts it: *the instinctive reaction is for the top to tell the middle what to do at the bottom.*

BUYING BACK IDEAS

So it was in the 1970s, when the managers of America's corporations began to sense that something was seriously wrong. The news was beginning to trickle-in that we were increasingly in competition with a model that used *everyone*, especially hourly employees, in quality improvement and ongoing problem-solving.

So, when management turned its attention to the problems of quality and worker alienation, it reached for its basic assumptions about motivation - the combination of carrot and stick. There *had* to be some extrinsic motivator that would work. And across the country, workplace to workplace, one of the more remarkable motivational strategies emerged in full bloom: the suggestion program.

We are so used to the idea, the words have lost their impact. But consider how ludicrous it was: this was a strategy of buying back each of those alienated employees, idea by idea. They are not "with" the organization for say, $25,000 a year in salary and benefits. But for $50 an idea, they are going to *drive* toward the success of the venture!

"The trouble was that no one had told the troops anything had changed."

Then across the nation, we kept score: average number of suggestions per employee, dollars saved, awards given. Some good short-term numbers. And nothing moved. It was over before the programs were fully set up in many places.

It was a remarkable strategy, and deeply embedded in the pathology. At least, it was an early recognition that everyone in the organization could be thoughtful.

MIDDLE MANAGEMENT MUST BE THE PROBLEM

Next, it occurred to top management that maybe middle management was the problem. In executive suites around the country words like "sensitivity" and "participation" emerged. Executives who six-months earlier had been blaming unions for the decline of Western civilization began to complain: "Our middle managers don't know how to manage participatively. We need to teach them." So, organizations began a significant training intervention aimed at the middle grid.

Throughout the 1970s armies of middle managers trooped off to Chicago and New Haven and other places to learn how to manage participatively. And two weeks later they came back to Tarrytown or South Bend and tried to apply what they had learned.

The trouble was that *no one had told the troops* anything had changed. Union and management were still adversarial, the workers were still alienated. There was still no open information flow, no substantive change in integration structures, no redefining of pay and promotion criteria, no change in attitudes from the top leadership...and yet the middle grid was supposed to move out, "participatively." Those who tried it got their heads handed to them, and vowed "never again."

Courses in participative management skills are still found in most of the training catalogs. The American Management Association (AMA) and others make millions teaching them, developing personal management "style profiles," and teaching Theory-Y approaches. Corporations with their consultants stage huge events around participation, listening activities, and training, and congratulate themselves that at least this piece has been fixed. It is the old visit to the parts store, pointless as ever.

Training strategies, in general, are vulnerable to the piecemeal fallacy. They tend to teach a needed skill, and then insert it in an organization that cannot tolerate it because the overall system has not moved. Participative management may have been light-years ahead of the suggestion box strategy, but it was a glaring anomaly in the hierarchial Steady State. A hopeful intervention lost its way for the time being.

PIECEMEAL TACTICS

Then, in the late 1970s, out of the defense industry came a wonderful new idea. Instead of trying to *buy* the troops back, companies like Lockheed decided that what the workers wanted was...information and control. They began moving away from manipulation of reward and punishment, toward powerful *intrinsic* motivators, in a strategy of giving teams information and some control over their own work.

This fundamental change was the creation of Quality Circles. Teams of workers were allowed to meet and problem-solve as part of their day-to-day functioning. Despite all the previous false starts, and all their anger, suspicion, and bad history, the amazing thing is that workers took to it powerfully and enthusiastically. The idea moved across the country, and practically every workplace was touched by the process.

The tragedy is that this wonderful movement was happening within the old military/ecclesiastical steady state, and no one had told the people at the top and middle that things had to change. *They* certainly weren't going to relinquish their control of information and power, nor move quickly and openly at the stimulus from below. And after four or five years, in workplace after workplace, you would hear a variation of this story,

"...many managers who latched onto his ideas simply wanted a quick fix."

"Yeah, we handed in a proposal, and we heard eighteen months later that they turned it down." The quality circle process rose quickly and broadly, but within six or seven years it withered away.

TOP DOWN TOTAL QUALITY

By now we had been through the failures of Suggestion Programs, Participative Management Training, and Quality Circles. Managers were understandably skeptical of yet another solution, but they were still willing to give it a try. And then, out of Japan, came Total Quality Management and its colorful and charismatic exponent, W. Edwards Deming. It sounded exactly right.

Total Quality is founded on a technical process of constant improvement coupled with careful measurement. Deming understood that this is an entire system, but many managers who latched onto his ideas simply wanted a quick fix. So they took his training, and plugged it into systems that hadn't addressed their basic pathologies. It presupposed people wanted to help, could talk about the short-fall without danger, and middle management wanted to listen. Not good assumptions in Steady State One. Another visit to the parts store.

The overriding lesson of all of these stories is that the remedies look dangerously like the dysfunctions that they are meant to heal. *They are almost always imposed from above, driven in isolated and unintegrated fashion, focused on short-term quantitative results, and seldom if ever involve the people who do the work.* The net result is often further dysfunction and deeper anger and frustration.

JUMP HIGHER OR ELSE

This is the profile of attempted reform and renewal in the private sector. What about the public sector? When the full torque of restructuring comes to public education, will it be any different? Or will we simply begin the process of change out of the same failed management orthodoxy? State legislatures are working hard on the issue, but the early reports are not encouraging.

A look at one 1991 case in Iowa gives an inkling of what the key elements of education restructuring might be. The Business Roundtable, a group of well meaning private corporations, commissioned a $400,000 study of public education in the state.

After the state board establishes schools and school districts' performance goals and assessment processes in Iowa, this type of recommendation follows:

> *"In evaluating the performance by a school, I recommend that you establish a threshold level of performance that will be deemed satisfactory.*
>
> *In schools in which the proportion of successful students actually declined but by less than 5%, the school staff would lose both one year of longevity pay and one cost-of-living increment."*

(Hornbeck, D. "First Draft of Recommendations on the Iowa Initiative for World Class Schools")

The various key actors including the teacher's union, the Iowa State Education Association, the School Administrators of Iowa, the Iowa Department of Education and others, were not significantly involved in developing this plan. Therefore, they were able to forestall a good deal of its thrust. As a matter of fact, these groups began their own collaborative learning model, based on listening to schools and districts as they started the long restructuring process.

From the beginning, the problem with legislated reform has been that no one reflects on the state of the present system. It is as though it makes no difference whether a district is rural, suburban, or urban; if adversarial relationships exist; what types of resources are available; and how a district or a state system is affected by community special interest groups and pressure groups that make day-to-day functioning an adventure at best. Too often, legislatures simply *demand required improvements* in test scores, add some carrot/stick language, involve none of the major actors, and wait for something to happen. It will be a long wait.

And from the wings, there increasingly is another voice that says, "Walk away from the whole system and its failures and use the resources to do it some other way. Trust a good competitive model from the private sector."

It's easy to invent wonderful models in isolation, apart from the real communities, parents, teachers, and children, and existing school systems. But we are not starting from scratch. The issue is how to find ways to change the huge system of public education we have in place. General Motors can come up with a splendid option in Saturn. But can any number of Saturns do anything for the core of the business at Pontiac, Oldsmobile, Cadillac or Chevrolet?

The countless false starts use scarce resources and greater disillusionment. But worse, they use up precious time. To move to the fundamental redesign of public education, *these* underlying issues need to be considered:

1.   ***Every organization is a single system*** - a state of organizational existence. Touch one part (a classroom, a principal, a significant piece of the curriculum), and you touch it all. You cannot design piecemeal or isolated solutions.

2.   Not only is this a deeply interconnected state, ***it is also fixed in position,*** powerfully and intricately. Try to change one piece, and the total system will slowly or violently pull the change back to its former Steady State. Strong reactive forces hold the system in place - and change must take place against them.

3.   In the Western world, there is a classic model for the Steady State. ***It is the traditional, organizational pyramid.*** Its characteristics are that it is top down, authoritarian, layered in hierarchy, gridded into silos, and restricts the flow of information and autonomy.

4.   The consequences of this form of organization are ***four major dysfunctions***:

a.   *It is a non-listening system* that cannot retrieve its own data nor learn from it.

b.   *It is a non-integrated system* in which groups work in specialized teams, and these teams and the individuals within them compete for power, position, and resources.

c.   *It is driven by short-term, quantitative measurements* that lead to dangerous miscalculations of the actual situation because they do not take into account the qualitative aspects of performance.

d.   *It cannot, by its very nature, sustain the energy, talent, and commitment of those who actually do the work.*

All change happens against this Steady State. All the pieces of the present system are interconnected. All the people in this system know a good deal about the problems and don't like the results. Yet they will resist the change. The system is us. We will resist the change we dream of and desperately pursue. It is the deep paradox of systems-change at the personal or organizational level. To design reform successfully, strategists must design *against* the pathology, and heal the system as it restructures itself.

Chapter Six: Paradoxes and Safe Havens

When starting any process of systemic change - whether it is school restructuring or family therapy - you need to know something about that particular system: what it looks like, how it got there, how the players interact. All of that is a precondition to any kind of change strategy.

A therapist won't begin by saying, "Here's how to be a more patient father" or "Let's work on your self-esteem." She will ask you to help her understand exactly what goes on in your particular world and how it was formed, and in the process of opening that up, you will begin to understand it yourself.

Now, you would think that, after you had gotten some insight, you could jump up one day and say, "Oh ho! I understand! Now I can go be a patient father." But, it doesn't work that way. In fact, the first law of systems is that: *Even if you understand the problem, the system will fight like mad to hold itself where it is.* That's the opening paradox of systemic change.

There is a lot of confusion around this inability of a system to act on its own data. In Family Systems Therapy work, for example, you'll find a curious pattern:

The family knows what's wrong.

They know what it is doing to them.

They *hate* it.

And, they can't get out of it.

The system is locked-in relationally, the players are locked into their roles. They are not in this mess because they are unaware, or because they like it. They are locked in because it is a *system.*

Very often when we get into a change process and it doesn't move, and as a matter of fact it resists strongly, our tendency is to say, "There must be devils here." And then we find devils all over the place...greedy unions, power hungry board members, uncaring teachers, uninvolved parents, controlling managers.

> **"...the first law of systems is that: Even if you understand the problem, the system will fight like mad to hold itself where it is."**

There's no shortage of these devils, but it is a waste of time and energy to look for them. This system is just us, and we are doing the best we can.

So, the first piece of data you have going in is the knowledge that this thing is not going to be a piece of cake. This system is going to fight like mad. It doesn't know what else to do and blaming will not help.

BUILDING A SCAFFOLD FOR THE CHANGE

There is a second paradox to systems change. On the one hand, you must have *a systemic strategy*. You can't move the thing piece by piece. On the other hand, you can't move it all at once. The way you move a Steady State is to "torque" the roles and relationships to create such unbearable tension at one place or another that the entire system suddenly slips, realigns, and finds itself in a different place. All of this happens in fits and starts, and while it is happening the Steady State system doesn't function very well.

It is a tough paradox, knowing you can't just change a piece, and you can't move it all at once either. But what makes these small changes different from a pilot program or a visit to the parts store is that you learn to link them somehow to the whole.

You must have a place to pull it back, where the system can learn. The reason you go back each week for therapy is so you can talk through what worked and what didn't. You create a moment, an event, but especially a "place" where the system can learn.

This is not a replacement for the everyday working structure. You don't live your life in a therapist's office, and you can't stop running a school district. But you need this safe place where you can get together, look at the structure, talk about it, and figure out together how to do it better.

**"This is the final paradox in restructuring an organization....
You design against the weakness."**

Within this "shadow structure," the various actors can try new behaviors and ideas without completely abandoning the existing Steady State. If you don't have this safe place where you can talk straight and tough and honestly, you won't get meaningful change.

All of this begins in a moment of careful diagnosis of the existing Steady State. The first critical decision in school reform is to determine where the system is. It is not a segment such as schedule or curriculum. It is not an individual school. It is not even an individual district. The "system" in the United States, is the state. We have fifty quite distinct systems, as a matter of fact.

The question really is, "Where does the thing I am trying to move, begin and end? Where does it cease being held in place by other parts?" That is where the system begins.

You need to begin by asking, at every point of the system, "How is it working? Where is the slippage?" Every system is unique, and however much it shares the general characteristics of the Western organizational model, its particular dysfunctions, as well as its strengths are unique. By understanding the blockages, you can begin to form a strategy for change. (Appendix D)

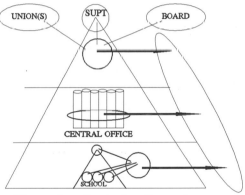

Even then, after you have identified the dysfunctions, you won't have the "answer" in terms of new structures or functions. In fact, if you did know the answer, the worst thing you could do would be to implement it.

Figure 6. Beginning Systemic Change: A Diagnostic Moment

Dismantling and directly replacing pieces may give speed and some early clarity. But, such a solution is usually dictated top down, and often a single group's version of the answer. The solution they come up with is generally a new, improved iteration of the old basic pathology. It comes without involvement and without the organization learning to learn. Even when you understand the problem, you can't fix it...the system has to heal itself.

This is the final paradox in restructuring an organization. You design *against the weakness.*

You create the pressure toward movement by deliberately laying over a shadow structure against the toughest dysfunctions. That creates the greatest pressure on the organization, and it's how it learns to heal itself.

At Ford in the late 70s the toughest issue was the bitter, deeply distrustful relationship with the UAW. It was a situation where no movement was possible, because there was no place for a dialogue to begin. So Peter Pestillo, Ford's top labor executive, and Don Ephlin, the UAW's vice president for Ford, decided to begin to travel together. They went everywhere together, as a team, to plants, to meetings all over the United States. They listened together, to each other's constituencies, as well as their own, and they spoke to those constituencies, always together. They created a sort of imagery of the joint relationship through their personal partnership, and along the way they learned to respect and listen to each other as well. It was a deliberate design at the point of pain, against the pathology.

In a school, where mistrust between the community and the administration is the major issue, you might begin to deal with it by making sure that parents were present at every major event, every meeting, every challenge. Within the discomfort of that presence, the learning and the healing could begin.

Generally, the greatest dysfunctions turn out to be typical of the pathologies of the Western organizational model: non-listening, and non learning organizations; poorly integrated organizations; with minimal communication and collaboration; short-term and quantitative values to the exclusion of all others; and the alienation and distrust of life at the bottom of the pyramid.

Once the diagnosis has identified the pattern of dysfunctions unique to that particular organization, you can begin to change the organizational frame. For example, if one critical problem seems to be integration, you might create as many temporary or shadow configurations as made sense, to force at least some horizontal meeting, sharing, and problem-solving. The goal would be to create stress on the separate silos, collapse the separateness, and create a need-to-know across the system. Eventually, this would create tremendous tension as it comes up against the resistant system, and something would have to move.

A design for change, then, is not a series of good ideas for how to do things better. It is a series of steps that lead to something else:

1. Understand the system-in-place and its dysfunctions.

2. Begin to design the scaffold or temporary structures that require opposite behavior or processes.

3. Create "moments" in which key leadership in the organization must reflect together on these activities, the stresses that have arisen, and what is going on between the new structures and the old.

4. Redesign more permanent structures based on these learnings.

The place to begin this process is with a deeper understanding of the system and the intricate web of relationships that hold it in place. Listening is not a one-time diagnostic event, but needs to be a way of life in the organization. It is a way to hear itself, the strong and the weak parts; and over the fear and the blaming, gather all the major actors to listen more intently, not just to the content of the issue, but to the way we listen and learn as well.

"A design for change, then, is not a series of good ideas for how to do things better. It is a series of steps that lead to something else..."

Chapter Seven: The Educational System and Its Boundaries

If you are going to use the word "system" as the major grounding to plant the question of educational restructuring, then it requires some further development. The first issue of systems-thinking is that the critical phenomena are *not* the individual parts, but how they fit together. This is a network of relationships deeply interconnected. Each one of the "sub-systems" is somehow defined by the position of the others. So, when you touch one thing -- such as the authority of the principal or the responsibility of a teacher -- you touch all the others.

Most of the failure of efforts at change come about because this delicate balance is not taken into consideration. Worker empowerment without redefinition of management's role, or middle manager retraining without a change in union-management relationships in the private sector is paralleled in public education by fast and loose descriptions of site-based decision making by parents and teachers with no acknowledgment of its profound systemic repercussions.

To begin understanding a particular web of relationships, you need a language and framework that lets you delineate the parts and their relationships to each other. There is no common term in the English language, but the closest is the word "boundary." "Boundary" is meant to connote both barrier and connection -- which is how these parts relate to each other.

THE SIX BOUNDARIES

To illustrate the boundary concept, we can use the example of a typical school district. There usually are six boundaries or subsystems within a school district. They are:

Boundary One: The Anchors
...the school board, the superintendent and central administrative cabinet, and the executive or bargaining committee of the union(s)

Boundary Two: **The Teachers, Support Staff, Students**

Boundary Three: **The Principals**

Boundary Four: **The Information System**

Boundary Five: **The Central Office and Specialties**

Boundary Six: **The Parents and Community...The External Environment**

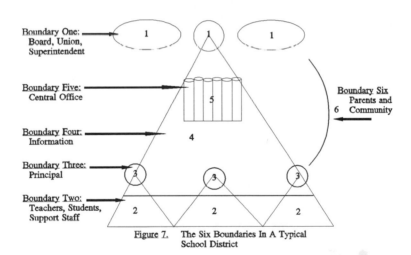

Figure 7.   The Six Boundaries In A Typical School District

Each of these boundaries plays a unique and essential role within the larger system.

"Most of the failure of efforts at change come about because this delicate balance is not taken into consideration."

BOUNDARY ONE: THE ANCHORS

This comprises three major players whose jobs, morally and legally, are to *anchor* the system from the top.

1. The elected school board expresses the educational goals of the community, its dreams, its fears, and its limitations, and translates that into policy directions.

2. The *administrative leadership team* is responsible for taking the policy directions of the board and the resources allocated by the community to organize the highest quality and most efficient delivery of public education.

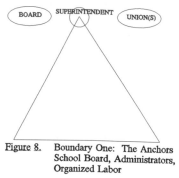

3. The *organized labor leaders* are elected to represent their members and their rights within the work setting.

Figure 8. Boundary One: The Anchors School Board, Administrators, Organized Labor

Each of the three anchor positions of Boundary One represent *distinct legal and moral obligations.* Often the full achievement of one group's goals may appear to be at the expense of another. This may result in an interesting exercise in balance of power, with two of the groups linked in a temporary alliance and the third temporarily excluded.

These are, however, uncertain, uneasy, and unstable liaisons in which no party feels secure.

"You must find a way to move these often adversarial relationships toward a more trusting, collaborative, and supportive relationship that frees the rest of the system to act differently, even as they retain their separate functions."

There is, however, one thing certain about Boundary One. If you want to achieve any significant change within the larger system, you must find a way for the anchors to move with you. You must find a way to move these often adversarial relationships toward a more trusting, collaborative, and supportive relationship that frees the rest of the system to act differently, even as they retain their separate functions.

BOUNDARY TWO: TEACHERS, STUDENTS AND SUPPORT ROLES

Boundary Two includes the folks who do the real work of the system: the teachers, the support staff, and the students. In coal mining companies, miners dig the coal, and in schools teachers teach and children learn. It's the bottom of the pyramid. In the classic Western model, you would expect this level to be uninformed, unempowered, disenfranchised, and alienated from the system. There would be little decision making role or access to critical information. Responsibility and authority would reside elsewhere. How does it look in a school?

One of the more deadly games in this type of system is the one surrounding responsibility. The higher echelons have been taught that *they* are responsible for the quality and efficiency of "those below." To handle this, they erect fairly complicated methods of monitoring

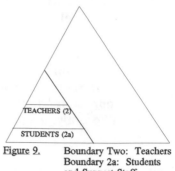

Figure 9.   Boundary Two: Teachers
Boundary 2a: Students
and Support Staff

and controlling, and they attempt to evaluate, with punishment and blame providing the context.

All this is called "evaluation."

But ordinarily any real work is hard to evaluate at its core, so the rules tend to touch only superficial facets. This is doubly true of education. As the rules and regulations multiply at state, local, and building levels, those doing the work and being evaluated withdraw from the system, away from open dialogue around the deeper issues, and eventually away from their own responsibility. Fear is at work.

"As the rules and regulations multiply...those doing the work...withdraw from the system."

The unique worker in education is the student. His or her work of learning is, of course, the real work, and all others are present to support this effort.

Yet, who is held responsible for this effort? All you have to do to answer that is look at who directs, controls, monitors, evaluates, rewards and punishes in this particular pyramid. It soon becomes clear that it is the adults who have the information, the power, and by extension, the responsibility. Predictably, too many students display the same attitudes as workers in an industrial enterprise: hopelessness, powerlessness, anger, sullenness, and finally deep alienation.

It may seem curious to group the teacher and the student together in a single categorization. But as you look at the two types of workers at the bottom of the educational pyramid, you will see that both are powerless, and both have had responsibility for their performance taken out of their hands, and assumed by those "above."

BOUNDARY THREE: THE PRINCIPAL

"You represent the high command, but you live and die with the troops."

In the classic organizational pyramid, authority and strategy are held at the top. The folks at the bottom do as they are told, more or less, well or badly, and maintain a sullen silence. There is enormous slippage between the command and control center and the bottom level. They cannot speak openly and honestly to one another. Hence, often they do not fit. So the model creates a shock absorber: the middle manager. These men and women live in the middle and absorb the shocks, making a system that doesn't fit together somehow function.

The middle manager in this model lives in a no-man's land. He or she is not part of either world. If the command sees you aligned with the troops, they say "Looks like we don't have the right person to translate our strategies." If those under you see you aligned with the top, they turn on you in an even more deadly way. We lost a lot of second lieutenants in Vietnam, and not

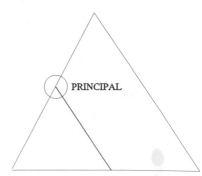

Figure 10: Boundary Three: The Principal

all of them were killed by enemy fire. It is a schizophrenic existence. You represent the high command, but you live and die with the troops. It is truly life in the middle.

The good ones interrupt the constant stream of requests and demands from above, soften the rage and frustration from below, and mediate the tough issues between the two levels. They shelter the troops, and when a command comes down that can't be avoided, they call their troops together and say "Here is one we cannot dodge. What are we going to do?" And the troops say "Okay, let's figure this one out." And they help come up with a design that lets them all live.

The middle-manager position is always present in this type of organization. In school systems they are called principals.

These middle managers of public education have an additional responsibility in this already schizophrenic existence. We say to them, "Screen the external customer - teacher interface as well. Protect this place and its work from unreasonable demands." In the end, the principal finds his or her role to be one of damage control, or managing the negative. It is often an unenviable life.

BOUNDARY FOUR: THE INFORMATION SYSTEM

Boundary Four is the information system developed to answer the essential question, "How are we doing?" Every functioning system must have a clear set of objectives and a way of gauging its performance. In the traditional model, the objectives are set at the top and sent down in the form of specific directives

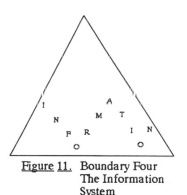

Figure 11. Boundary Four
The Information System

to the middle. Along with the directives, the middle manager is charged with aggregating small pieces of information that measure the performance of the workers in fulfilling their assignments. Applying these measurements --and they are purely quantitative -- the middle manager sends up a stream of reports aggregating the results of the work done by the troops so that the top can form a picture of "how well we are doing." It is always retrospective; it is always aggregate; and its always for the benefit of the

command and control center. It is a classic response to the
pathology of the top down, fear-driven, controlling pyramid
frustrated by its inability to reach all the way to the bottom.

"**The information that is accessible to the teacher is
too often not helpful, not timely, and has very little
to do with what is actually going on in his or her
classroom.**"

In a factory, these goals and measures are usually
designed by process flow specialists, who impose a set of
operator-proof, uniform, invariable processes. The worker
neither "owns" the goals or measures, nor understands how
they were arrived at. They belong to someone else, and
that someone else has got to figure it out, worry about it,
and enforce it.

In a typical school, Boundary Four very often exists for
the benefit of the "central office." The information that is
accessible to the teacher is too often not helpful, not timely,
and has very little to do with what actually is going on in
his or her classroom. As a result, "someone else" is
responsible for the work, and the teacher and the students
are there only to carry it out. If you are going to redesign
an educational system so that it places responsibility for
quality where it belongs -- with those who do the work --
then *they* have to help create the vision, the goals, the
measures that are relevant to them. What's more, Boundary
Four is continuous. You must constantly be working on it
to keep the system listening, learning, and improving --
pushing and pulling itself.

A fundamental problem with the classic pyramid is that

Boundary Four, the Information System, usually exists only for those above, and is dependent on the top-down control structure to sustain it and enforce it.

You know you have a problem when you walk into a school and you ask "Who is setting the goals in here?" and the folks say "I don't know." Or, you ask "What are the goals?" and they answer "Oh, they are around here somewhere. There is a piece of paper. It's yellow, I think. They handed it out on September 15th." Who is setting the goals, and does anyone trust the mechanism or the ultimate test? Ask the students to tell you who is responsible for their behavior and learning. It is probably as good a test as you can apply to gauge the health of a school.

BOUNDARY FIVE: THE CENTRAL OFFICE AND SPECIALISTS

In a world of complex tasks, every system needs some specialists. In a steel mill they might need specialized skills in materials handling, or molecular engineering. In the educational world, these are the experts in curriculum design, developmental psychology and special education. In neither world do you need these high expertise folks at the point of delivery every day. But if you are in trouble or if you are thinking about a fundamental change in the content of your work, you draw on their skills. These are essential skills.

The problem is what we have done with them. We have situated them high up in the system, where they become part of the command structure. Suddenly, their job

isn't just to help and support the re
monitor, control, police, and evalu

It often feels, in the
classroom, that the students and
the teachers are not there to
collaborate in their difficult work
of learning, but that the
classroom is there to satisfy the
discrete, unintegrated or even
opposed special requirements of
the command units above. *Their*
requirements become the focus,
not the needs of the classroom.
It is a system gone haywire. A
system in reverse.

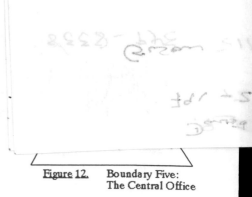

Figure 12.   Boundary Five:
               The Central Office

The special expertise located in Boundary Five is
absolutely necessary for excellence in the system. It should
be the place where integration and strategy flow, to produce
a quality product.   The issue is how to use these special
skills to support, inform, and improve without their
becoming a separate set of demands.

**"The issue is how to use these special skills to support,
inform, and improve without their becoming a separate
set of controlling demands."**

BOUNDARY   SIX: PARENTS   AND   THE COMMUNITY

Boundary Six is the external relationship of the school
system with its critical environment -- the community in

which it lives and to which it offers its service. It is a place of tension, and at times antagonism. The relationship between customer and system, always dynamic, has become more and more heated in recent years. In its worst iteration, the major question becomes how to keep the customer at a distance amid increasingly shrill demands for access and input.

"If a system begins to move in the direction of decentralized decision making and Site Councils, this Boundary will have to change significantly."

Often, the external group is so diverse and so demanding that the instinctive response is to treat it as a threat. This further heightens customer frustration and raises the level of shrillness, further increasing the self-protectiveness of the system.

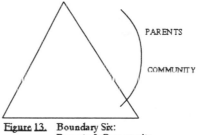

Figure 13. Boundary Six: Parents & Community

The real question, however, is how to keep the listening sharp with respect to the customers' needs and requirements and still maintain the integrity of the system. Right now one of the major openings is at Boundary One in terms of providing access to the community at the school board level. But if a system begins to move in the direction of decentralized decision making and site councils, this Boundary will have to change significantly. Boundary Six, where the school, the principal, and the staff meets the parents and the community, will take on a dramatically different look.

SUMMARY

The central idea of systems theory is that an organization, a school system, is all one, in the sense that if you want to move any part, you understand that you must move the whole thing.   Each of the Six Boundaries represents a significant element or subsystem of the larger system.   Any significant change to one Boundary means a significant change for every other part.   That makes the process of change highly complex and resistant.   But it also means that you can create considerable torque on tough systems in place.   If your tactics are consistent at each Boundary, then the pressure on one place will create other pressures elsewhere.   It is a source of powerful energy because pressure applied at one Boundary can dislodge another resistant Boundary.

In developing a working strategy, you need to hold the total system of a school or a district in your mind at any given moment, while at the same time focusing this moment's particular tactic on a single Boundary or subsystem.   It is a total system, with each part interconnected, but very often the tactics require changing one or two Boundaries, little by little, in a very focused manner.

Chapter Eight:
Anchors At
Boundary One
- Setting Sail

Nowhere are the risks of change greater than at Boundary One. It is here - with the board, the top administrative team, and the union leadership - that the entire system is anchored. Each group has a definite moral and legal responsibility within this system. Somehow, they must find a way to honor their commitments, holding to fundamentals, while at the same time being open to change. It is a paradox of anchoring and at the same time allowing movement.

The direction of the change in restructuring is clear enough. It is a movement of responsibility, information, empowerment and appropriate decision-making deep into the organization, to the level of the school, to the student and to the teacher. It also involves changing much of the monitoring and controlling that has traditionally been done higher up in the organization to a new activity of support and consultation.

It is easy to agree on the value of this type of empowerment in the abstract. But in the beginning, the actual process represents enormous risk for each of the anchors, and requires considerable courage.

For the *school board*, the danger, of course, is that in this whole process the decentralization and movement of power into the schools and classrooms will break up the uniform direction that a central school board has traditionally been expected to provide. Moving from a role of centralized policy making to a policy of open information flow and shared decision making is even more traumatic. In a community, this can create anxiety, suspicion, and down-right resistance, particularly from individuals who have been elected by special interest groups to protect certain areas and topics at all costs.

For the top administrators, restructuring represents a direct challenge to one of the basic tenets of management. Anyone professionally trained as a middle or upper-level manager in this country has been taught at some point that one of the fundamental roles of the manager is to protect, at all costs, against any significant erosion of "management rights." The prospect of moving decision making to the delivery point, to those who do the work and to the customer, looks like the worst of all possible worlds. Never mind the rhetoric, what it looks like up close is loss of control, erosion of management rights and responsibilities, and a kind of self- inflicted diminution in which you move decision making elsewhere, but are probably going to continue to be held responsible for what occurs. It doesn't sound politically smart, either.

As for the *organized-labor leadership,* restructuring challenges the very role of the union. Flowing from its position as protector of the rights of individuals within the system comes a fundamental principle that says that the union is the single vehicle for employees to deal with management in any fundamental way. Otherwise, the

"The prospect of moving decision-making to the delivery point, to those who do the work and to the customer, looks like the worst of all possible worlds."

theory goes, management will be able to manipulate practices in arbitrary and individualized contexts. Telling a responsible union leadership that it should trust management not to abuse this flexibility is to go against years of tradition and belief. In fact, as management inevitably moves in this direction of empowerment of employees, the union is really either left with opposing this step, or as with the UAW at Saturn, joining the effort completely and making the shift in decision-making a shared partnership of problem-solving and improvement. It is, after all, the only real long-term guarantor of security and dignity.

CALLING THE QUESTION

"So, begin by calling the question with each anchor: In the face of these risks, why are you interested in restructuring and decentralization?"

An understanding of these enormous exposures is needed from the point of view of each anchor when you talk about restructuring or site based decision making. If you don't, you will approach this entire process unrealistically and without the ability to address openly the often unexpressed fears.

So, *begin by calling the question with each anchor*: "In the face of these risks, why are you interested in restructuring and decentralization?"

There must be something in it for each of the anchors. What is that motive, and how can you plant it at the moral and legal level?

For organized labor, the issue around the country is "How do we renew ourselves?" Unions exist because there is a set of fundamental issues with respect to the rights of individual men and women in large work organizations. From the beginning, alongside pay and working conditions, it has been a question of respect.

Here is an opportunity for a union to find a path toward the deeper intrinsic motivators for its members. No organized labor group can declare itself against voice and empowerment for its members simply because it might lead to some lessened need for a protector. But to pursue the change *actively,* requires a higher form of courage. It calls for the union itself to understand what it means for its members to be empowered, responsible, responsive to the customer. The union would need enough confidence, ultimately, to say to its members, "We now have a new and additional role looking for opportunities to create richer work settings for you."

With respect to the management, the argument is equally powerful. If there were a significant possibility of delivering improved quality and efficiency by placing more information, more power, and more responsibility in the hands of teachers and students, you would have to consider it very carefully. It would be difficult to find a position behind "management rights" stating that, "Although it's true that restructuring would improve quality and efficiency, the loss of power is too high a price to pay."

For school boards, the argument is clear. They are elected to represent the dreams and desires of the community with respect to the education of its children. If schools are able to offer a process in which that community and its parents/customers were able to gain greater voice and influence on the delivery of education, who could argue against it?

The passion for quality and improvement surely is a powerful motivator to accept the risks of diversity. And risks there are, for each of the anchors. The beginning of an open dialogue comes when each of the other anchors begins to think not only about the exposure to themselves, but to the other actors involved.

TAKING THE GIANT LEAP

The final consideration is the issue of *systemic* versus personal change strategies. In education, the cult of the individual is very strong. Educational folklore is filled with the charismatic leader who can imprint a school or district. "The school is spectacular since she arrived as principal." "It's amazing how much the new superintendent has been able to accomplish in just a year." And, sometimes, it is true that restructuring occurs in schools or districts because individuals in key positions have learned to trust one another and share some common goals. But individuals come and go as do Board members, superintendents, union leaders. The work of changing a system is too important to make it dependent on who is sitting in the chair at that moment. Some other more institutional commitment is necessary.

A handshake deal is a wonderful thing, but it's far better to have this agreement in writing. There's always the chance that one day, three years later, you'll look up and the Board has changed, or the union leadership has changed, and someone says, "What is this restructuring stuff?"

And you say, "Oh, gee, the guys you just voted out wanted to do this!"

"When you're trying to produce a high trust statement in a low-trust environment, it's best to make it simple, and make it short."

School leaders want to be able to say, "On August 15, 1994, by a 7 - 0 vote, the board agreed to do this, and on August 19, all parties signed a Letter of Understanding that was incorporated into the union contract. That contract was voted on and accepted by the membership, and we've been carrying out those intentions ever since." Such documents lend some heft to the understanding, in case things change.

A long, involved adversarial document that protects everyone's interests doesn't help. On the contrary: *When you're trying to produce a high trust statement in a low trust environment, it's best to make it simple, and make it short.*

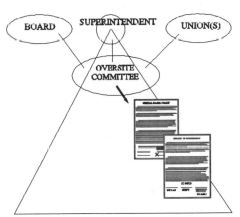

Figure 14. **Giving Permission: Signed Agreements & Policies**

The document need only include a paragraph of some general intent, a general protection of contract and personnel issues, a "safety net" clause to advise the other of possible withdrawal with adequate time to discuss the reasons, and a final paragraph that says either party is free to exit if it appears necessary to them. The object is to maintain a language of trust, openness, freedom, and change while giving some stability to the long-term effort. (Appendix A)

By far, the best process to achieve this is to explore restructuring together. An education or "design" committee with representation from all key positions in the school system is a solid way to begin. After sufficient exposure to the ideas, the board should vote on a simple resolution to proceed or not. The executive committee of the union and the administrative cabinet should have the same discussion. It is not enough for a policy board to mandate change; it is not enough for management to be given the responsibility and to try and drive it from above; and it is not enough for an organized labor group to demand this kind of right and voice for its members.

That is simply the playing out of old roles, and it won't succeed. Only if all parties are positive, and the anchors have *together* given permission to proceed, can the real work begin.

This careful, deep exploration is hard work, and you have to ask yourself, "why bother?" In fact, a lot of school districts have moved toward site-based decision making without going through the hassle of a long conversion process at Boundary One.

DEEP BUY-IN AT THE TOP

Typically, someone on the school board reads an article somewhere, and gets the other members of the board a bit interested. They then call in the management and say to them, "This sounds like good stuff. Why don't you try it somewhere." Management takes the union leadership out to lunch and says, "Hey, we are going to try this thing,

don't worry about it. Your people are really going to like
it." The union says, "Well, it sounds good, but just don't
touch the contract." Management says, "No problem."
And they're off and running.

About two years later, a couple of groups at
different sites around the district start taking this site-based
decision making seriously. They begin really moving,
making some changes, reaching out for significant
innovation. All of a sudden those anchors at the top start
screaming in unison "Stop!! What are you *doing*?" And,
the groups down in the schools say, "But you *told* us to do
it." And, the anchors say, "But we didn't mean *that*!"

> **"One must build a reflective structure for the three
> anchors to listen and learn together to sustain
> the linkage with the sites."**

It's not so much that they haven't *approved it*. But
they have not been learning *with* the sites. It's not enough
to give permission to do. The anchors have to understand,
on a very deep level, exactly what it is they have given
permission for. It takes time, and it seems an unnecessary
drag on moving ahead when the need for change is so clear
and urgent. But it's critical that the anchors must move
with the system as it begins to unstick. Otherwise, they'll
snap it back with all the power of a Steady State in flux.

Give it and then take it away, and then visit one of
those sites six months later and you will find a group of
very angry, very bruised people, and a very dysfunctional
school. The district will have missed a great opportunity,

and it will be a long while before someone gathers up the courage to try again.   A little more time invested at Boundary One could have prevented the whole debacle. One must build a reflective structure for the three anchors to listen and learn together to sustain the linkage with the sites. We will discuss that in Chapter Eleven.

Chapter Nine: Changes at the Core - Boundaries Two, Three, Four, and Five

BOUNDARY TWO: TEACHERS, STUDENTS, AND SUPPORT STAFF

"The difficulty is that, in changing Boundary Two, you will simultaneously have to change every other Boundary connected to it."

Everybody in this country is trying to change Boundary Two. There's not much disagreement that this is where the real work of the system takes place and that quality education depends on what happens between the teacher and the learner. So naturally, school districts focus their energy on fixing that.

87

The difficulty is that, in changing Boundary Two, school districts will simultaneously have to change every other Boundary connected to it.   New roles for the principal, the information system, and the central office will have to be developed and defined.   There is a deep linkage between all these sub-systems, and somehow districts must find a way to move power and responsibility to students and teachers while retaining the integrity and meaningfulness of the other positions.   This is no small challenge.

Right now, in most systems, principals are held responsible for the quality of teaching in their schools, and teachers are held responsible for students' work.   Both groups, in many ways, are driven by the demands of the information system and the central office.   Breaking that deadly linkage of responsibility for others is the only way to free individual teachers and learners to achieve quality. From superintendent to teacher, the key is not being responsible for others, but creating settings in which others can be responsible for themselves.

This does not mean abandoning norms and goals. We need them, actually more than ever in a decentralized system. The change comes in how standards are determined.

Traditionally, we have had a commitment to individual communities making their own choices about goals and measurement. The problem is that with all this enormous freedom and flexibility, we have gotten to the point where goals aren't really being set at any level, including at the school and in the classroom.   Retention rates and movement grade to grade are often the only "measurement."

For some students, the high school diploma has meant a very rigorous process with very careful kinds of measurement, four or five hours of work per night for four years, perhaps some independent study. For others it has meant that they have shown up for class most of the time during the four years, but there is no guarantee that they ever opened a book, wrote a paragraph, or reflected on an idea. The country as a whole, and taxpayers and parents in particular, are about to demand something more than this. The terrifying prospect is that it will lead to some national lockstep with respect to standardized goals, standardized testing, and standardized curriculum.

When Goodyear sells a tire to General Motors, say for the new Corvette, the specifications are non-negotiable. Goodyear beat out Michelin by promising to deliver a certain kind of dimension, tread, and long-term performance characteristic. Those specifications have to be honored wherever the tire is built - by a group of tire builders in Alabama or in a plant in Texas.

But down at Goodyear's plant in Gadsden, Alabama, they have about two hundred machines. Perhaps fifty are brand new, state-of-the-art. Fifty others are as much as 48 years old, rebuilt half a dozen times. Maybe another hundred have been picked up here and there from other plants. When Goodyear's vice president goes down to Gadsden and says, "I have wonderful news. We have sold this tire to General Motors and these are the specifications," he does not then go on to say "And here is how you will build these tires." He knows that within that very specific and inflexible set of requirements, there has to be enormous flexibility with respect to the judgment and expertise of the individual tire builder and the way the plant is organized to apply its own experience and teamwork to those very different machinery capabilities.

Similarly, within a school system, there should be certain non-negotiable norms and requirements. Some things, like Scholastic Aptitude Tests (SAT), or Advanced Placement (AP) requirements, are givens. There is also a common base of agreement with respect to what ought to be covered in a high school year of algebra or introductory chemistry. You can even predicate certain quality outcomes. But how these are delivered should be up to the site, the teacher, the student -- within the non-negotiables of the community, board, and professionals. Outcomes for a high school graduate should be crystal clear.

It is interesting that in France, where most decisions are highly centralized, the only national standard on reading is that children should be able to read by the age of 7. How they get there is entirely up to the individual teacher -- including methodology, curriculum, pace, and measurement. And even with an increasingly diverse student body, French schoolchildren read better than students in most other developed countries.

"The change will be in the quality, not the essential nature of the work."

This is not simply a Utopian argument for relinquishing authority across the board. There is a huge gamut of educational decisions made every day.

Some of those decisions clearly belong with the central office, and the board. Some belong at the site. Many more belong with the teachers and the children they work with. The movement comes in reconsidering *where* those decisions are made.

Empowering teachers may or may not require them to do things any differently. They may just do what they already know how to do, better, more responsibly and more creatively. They may feel safe and empowered enough to reach for new methods and material. In any case, when teachers are free to do that, the students will follow. The change will be in the quality, not the essential nature of the work.

BOUNDARY THREE: THE PRINCIPAL AS COORDINATOR

Someone is going to feel the real brunt of change, and that person lives at Boundary Three. Somehow, in this process of shifting responsibility, you must build a very different kind of role for the middle-manager.

> **"It is absolutely essential that this new role for Boundary Three be carved out at the same time Boundary Two begins to push against the old structure."**

For years, the middle manager in the private sector was the odd man out when empowerment moved down the organization. Eventually, the systems that ended up successfully transforming themselves discovered that the middle manager, far from being an anachronism, was really critical to freeing the rest of the organization. It's the same with schools.

It is absolutely essential that this new role for Boundary Three be carved out at the same time Boundary Two begins to push against the old structure. The new role has several components. In the first, the principal becomes the linch-pin who creates the processes in which people can talk to one another, sharing information across the silos, integrating all the different specialties.

The second component calls for the principal to act as system leader, helping the other actors identify and agree to the site's goals, and then keeping those goals visible and in focus for them at all times.

Building the goals and the mission is the critical breakthrough, because if you can do this you can get out of the role of controlling people. If you can stop controlling them, they can come alive. You are saying to the principal, "You are not responsible for what happens in this building and to the people in it. You no longer need to control and monitor their productivity and quality. But you *are* responsible for seeing to it that they have an environment in which they can take responsibility."

We have to get principals out of the role of trying to be responsible *for* teachers, because when they are they get everything wrong...angry people, dysfunctional schools.

**"The key is for all parties to agree about what they
want their goals to be, and then agree on who is
responsible for which part."**

When you walk into a steel mill and ask, "Who's responsible in this place for quality and productivity?" you will get two different kinds of answers. In the bad mills people will say, "That dummy over there with the tie." In the good mills they will say, "*We* are." The same thing is true in a big high school. Go into a cafeteria at lunch time, sit down with a group of the toughest, most boisterous kids, and ask them, "Who is responsible in this school for what you do?" If they point to some unhappy thirty-five-year-old in the corner and say, "That guy/woman over there," you know you are in trouble.

The key is for all parties to agree about what they want their goals to be, and then agree on who is responsible for which part. When I send my son off to college, I say to him "My responsibility is to find a big bag of money, and spend a large chunk of my life doing it, so that you can attend college. Now tell me what you think your responsibility is." That's his chance to step up to it unequivocally, and on his own terms.

The principal's role as internal coordinator and facilitator grows as more freedom passes to the individual teachers and classrooms. The job becomes one of looking for opportunities to form teams where appropriate, to augment communication where there is slippage or fuzziness around similar efforts in three or four classrooms, and also to look for similarities that begin to occur across the system that need to be heightened and punctuated. This may not look too different from what some really fine principals have been doing for many years, but the dramatic change here is that the *teachers* are the initiators. They have deliberately said to these principals, "This is what we need from you, and this is what *we* empower *you* to do for *us*."

One thing does not change. The principal is still the one in the middle, sandwiched between the central system and the site. The difference now is that the principal will be less a middle-management pass-through of requirements set at the top, and more one whose job it is to make the site aware of issues, and to advocate for specialized resources available from the central office to enrich and expand what is occurring at the site. It is still a role of linking to the central system, but it is no longer as controller and manager. It is one of advocate and enabler.

Finally, the principal assumes a new, richer role. As greater and greater flexibility begins to emerge from the sites themselves, more attention must be spent on linking similar sites. This linkage should occur not only horizontally, but throughout the chain of education, so that what is learned at fifth-, sixth-, and seventh-grade is acknowledged, understood and deepened in the high school. Within this new paradigm a great deal of effort will have to go into cross fertilization of the sites in order to keep the deeper collaboration and coordination alive.

When you deliberately walk away from a top/down, more formally coupled system to one driven by a deeper understanding of its interdependency, the principal's role will emerge as that of deep coordinator within the site, coordinator school to school between principals one site to another, and as coordinator and enricher from the site to the central system, continuously looking for opportunities to engage the customer -- parent and community -- in positive ways.

BOUNDARY FIVE: CENTRAL OFFICE

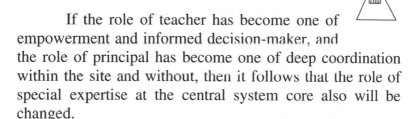

If the role of teacher has become one of empowerment and informed decision-maker, and the role of principal has become one of deep coordination within the site and without, then it follows that the role of special expertise at the central system core also will be changed.

Throughout the private sector in the 1980s came a growing realization that the energy being spent trying to control quality and performance at the point of delivery from above, was wasted effort. The powerful movement for the last ten years has been dismantling the long-term accretion of layers and layers of control. There   is   a somewhat brutal but probably accurate shorthand for this shift. You need about a third of the older system performing systemic control and monitoring processes, so that the total system understands how it is performing, and compares and integrates those separate pieces of data. You need another third of that expertise redistributed in some significant way, both structurally and functionally -- and probably physically as well -- to be close to the delivery in the field where the work is done. And, in the end, you will probably need about a third fewer men and women in the old control functions.

The same kinds of structural and functional changes will occur in school systems as you attempt to renew them using the system in place as a starting point. Long term accretion will be dismantled. The central control at Boundary Five will begin to redistribute its resources, retaining some responsibility for overall system collaboration, while sending its special expertise into the field in a consultative fashion. Ultimately the site probably will control a majority of its budget and its expenditures for the school.

As teachers take on more and more of the responsibility for what goes on in their classroom, they will have increasing need for some presence to deliver expertise and support on an as-needed basis. So the curriculum experts will be relocated "close" to the site to help enrich and create new approaches collaboratively with teachers and learners.

But if you dismantle the old system, what is it that drives the changing system constantly toward performance and improved quality?

"The old Steady State information system collects data to reward some people and punish others."

BOUNDARY FOUR:
THE INFORMATION SYSTEM

One of the better ways to answer this is to begin with the information system already in

place. In the Steady State, it's a top-down accountability
and goal-setting process, imposed on teachers and students
and driven by a reporting process.   That produces dry
mouths and clammy hands, and a great deal of easy
avoidance, but not much joy of learning or teaching. The
old Steady State information system collects data to reward
some people and punish others. Those who respond to its
imperatives feel that it has little to do with their work, let
alone its improvement. It is a distraction, artificial and
unintegrated and burdensome, but most importantly, never
owned by the men and women or the girls and boys who do
the work.

As districts work toward a new system, they can't
back off the collection of data, because they need that
information more than ever.   Boundary Four becomes the
key to the board's capacity to free the root of the system
If the new goal-setting and measurement system is built
well, with both clarity and involvement, so that all the
players trust it, *then* its possible to allow the schools and
the community to use their skill, energy, and vision to
achieve the goals. So the board must put in place an
authentic process involving community and professional
staff to create clear *goals, indicators, assessment,* and
public disclosures.

But the entire focus is different. You begin to build
a new, more authentic information system by going to <u>all</u>
of those who by rights should own it: the teachers, the
community, the parents, and the central administration and
school board.

For example, the board might say, "A 12th-grader should be able to read and analyze a 3,000-word article on health care from *The Wall Street Journal*. That is the level of achievement we expect."

"So the Board must put in place an authentic process involving community and professional staff to create clear goals, indicators, assessment, and public disclosures."

This particular blue-collar community, however, may be looking for something different for their kids. Those parents know that the largest employer in town tests all job applicants for both computer literacy and the ability to work in teams. They want their kids to graduate from high school capable of finding good jobs in that community. Somehow Boundary Four must reflect those hopes. So you keep going back and building and refining the goals so that they become more authentic, with deeper input from the community, and a constant ability to learn and improve. This will happen over time, in a series of iterations that get sharper and sharper. The first efforts will probably not look very different from the traditional measures. In fact, you could be running a parallel system while building the new one, keeping the old standards while building deeper kinds of assessment.

At the district and each site level, Boundary Four looks like a series of information pieces beginning with an overall mission statement. It incorporates whatever state and national requirements are relevant, and somehow also reflects the values and dreams of a particular community. It will have clarity as well, clearly drawing out a series of indicators connected to direct educational achievement. For instance, the board may have developed a mission statement along these lines:

The Two Rivers Public School District shall assist each student, commensurate with his/her abilities, to achieve the following:

A.   *Development of pride and motivation in personal effort and achievement.*

B.   *Competence in analytical thinking, problem-solving, decision-making, and creativity.*

C.   *Competence in the basic skills: reading, writing, communication (speaking and listening), and mathematics.*

D.   *Preparation for post-secondary school experiences including the "world of work," further formal education, direct education for employment, and appreciation of life-long learning.*

Two Rivers then added some specific, measurable, academic goals.

> *By the year 2000, students will leave grades four, eight, and twelve having demonstrated competency in challenging subject matter including English, mathematics, science, history, and geography; and every school will ensure that all students learn to use their minds well, so they may be prepared for responsible citizenship, further learning, and productive employment in our modern economy.*

Administers the State of Wisconsin Third Grade Reading Test.

Administers standardized achievement tests at grades 2, 3, 4, 5, 6, 7, and 8.

Provides opportunities for pupils for on-the-job training.

Source: Two-Rivers Public School District, Two Rivers, Wisconsin. (Appendix B)

At the school, the Site Council will have added its own piece. It might say, "We want to educate productive members of society, able to provide for themselves in a world that demands strong quantitative and analytic skills. Therefore, in this school we will require three years of computer training. Every one of our graduates must be able to write a coherent, well organized essay, reflecting some basic research that demonstrates the ability to use library tools and a computer data base."

"We also want to build citizens. We want to teach our children the value of community and community service. Therefore, we will stress service as part of the four years they spend here, and build that emphasis into our cognitive and behavioral curriculum. Before a student graduates, he or she will have to complete one hundred hours of direct community service, and write a paper on the experience."

In the classroom, that set of site goals translates into a particular curricular emphasis. The 11th-grade social science class, for example, might research questions on how service is manifested in communities around the country.

The literature course might include the autobiography of Albert Schweitzer or some of Tolstoy's writings.

Deliberately building the goal of service into its curriculum and structure, the school will build a culture in which service is honored and brings prestige and success. It is the same process by which today we instill competition and winning as values. There is surely room for both as reflections of the community's values.

"...in the process of sharing and discussing in an ongoing exchange, you build even deeper authenticity around your attempts to push yourselves, measure yourselves, and improve."

These iterations of Boundary Four will have to be built and continued in an ongoing process at the district and site levels as the system constantly works to renew itself. You are driving for an information system with constant evaluation that lets the school know where they are, where they're getting close, and where they're falling short, in a way that pushes the system and the people in it to ongoing improvement.

An information system at Boundary Four that brings with it ownership and authenticity is capable of breaking open the other frozen roles and relationships. No longer is there a hierarchy of one group commanding and being responsible for others. Instead, the goals and measures are "out there" in public and owned by all the major actors. And in the process of sharing and discussing in an ongoing exchange, you build even deeper authenticity around your attempts to push yourselves, measure yourselves, and improve.

Now, real quality management can begin. Those who do the work have taken responsibility; the special expertise is there to enrich and support; and a key group has been freed from a "no win" situation in the middle to an even more powerful position of coordinating and coaching. The customer is included in and begins to trust the process. You have begun to allow for diversity in how sites can get to mandated goals. Most important, you have unleashed the power, energy, and drive for continuous improvement of teachers and students who live in the system and relate to it.

Chapter Ten: The Student - The Key to Quality and the Ultimate Worker

Who, in the end, is at the very bottom of the educational pyramid? Who is the ultimate worker, the final station in the top/down command-control configuration? It is, of course, the student.

Every student understands that he/she is there to do the bidding of infinite layers of authority, to satisfy a set of requirements imposed from somewhere up in the hierarchy, inside and out, for some reason or another. As with any other Steady State organization, as soon as someone else has taken over the measurement, control, and goals, at that moment the caring and responsibility for the work pass from the worker to somewhere else in the system. What's left is anger, sometimes at a profound level.

"...like the hourly worker, the student responds, sometimes quietly, sometimes with a good deal of passion: I HATE IT!"

Like the hourly worker whose rage and alienation consumed him every day of his working life, the student hears the system say to him at every turn, "You are stupid. You don't care. And you can't be trusted." And, the danger is that like the hourly worker, the student responds, sometimes quietly, sometimes with a good deal of passion, "I HATE IT!"

In school after school you will find them -- angry, sullen, disenfranchised from the system.   The only difference between them and the typical steelworker is that they are still young enough to make a game out of it, to say, "Okay, how can we mess with it today?"

The tragedy is that teachers and principals take on the responsibility for children's learning for all the *right* reasons. It feels right to control, because you care. And the hardest thing for an educator to overcome is that sense of being personally responsible for the student's work and its quality.

The principal has already been told, "You are not responsible for controlling and monitoring what happens in this building. You are, however, responsible for creating a place where the people in this building can do their work."

You are also saying to the teacher, "You are not responsible for these children's learning. You are responsible for seeing to it that *they* can take responsibility." The real product is not so much the content that is absorbed, but the effort -- how hard these children work, and what kind of stamina and focus they bring to the learning. They are differently gifted, and in that lies some wonderful diversity. You can build measures that include how fully they are pushing themselves to their own individual capacities, along with the more objective measures of how well they score.

This process implies a qualitative alliance between the parent and the teacher. The feedback around student performance now changes, focusing on how to help the child push against his or her own individual indicators.

The teacher might say to a parent, "Teddy is really doing well. I know he is not in the 95th percentile - in fact he is at the 85th percentile - but he is working hard and I couldn't be more pleased with his progress. That's the way I talk to him. If you can keep encouraging him to do as well as he has and keep putting out the effort, he will have a great year. Don't worry about how well he's done in the overall rankings. He's learning how to tackle tough material and master it, and that's what counts."

RANKING: ONE AGAINST THE OTHER

Of course, this runs smack into our national obsession with numbers as a way of ranking, and the entire frame we place around measurement itself. If you look at the beginning experience in any school, usually around third- or fourth-grade, the encounter with grades is fundamentally the same. It is the experience of being *ranked* against others. It becomes an enormously threatening activity, particularly if a student is struggling in certain areas. Insidiously, the measurement system begins to curtail not only the joy of learning, but the ownership, the openness to explore, and the ability to work collaboratively with others.

What is left is a deep sense that the other student is at some fundamental level the enemy in an enormously competitive and rigged system in which some are better than others. The fundamental work of the schools seems to be to establish as precisely as possible that ranking and declare it to the world. That is first and foremost the question colleges ask of individual students when they come out of high schools: SAT scores, rank in class, and grade-point average constitute who you are. The computers only allow consideration of you as a person *if* the numerical projection is "worth it." It says everything about what it is we think we are about in our schools. Who asked the schools to focus their prime efforts into sorting society into levels of academic skills, rather than to teach those skills?
The question really is: even if schools *have to* perform this set of ranking tasks, how can they focus on deeper issues, lay in devices, and set a tone for the more important work of the learning experience?

For several years I taught Latin and Greek in a high school that had absolute ranking by class. The classes were identified as A Class, B Class, C Class and D Class and students were assigned according to their grade-ranking with each other. I taught Latin to the A and B classes for two years, and the classes won national competitions both years. For the next two years I taught the D classes. At the end of the year, we didn't make it in any state competitions, and as a matter of fact, we didn't even enter any. But if you had asked me where the learning was really going on, I would have told you that the most successful work was done in the D classes.   On an objective measure, perhaps they did not perform as well as the A and B groups, but when you looked at the effort, and the progress that was made by the D groups those years, there is no question that they were superlative.

"I am not responsible for your learning.   I already know it. I'll help every way I can. But it is your issue and challenge. Yours individually and together."

THE LEARNER AS RESPONSIBLE FOR LEARNING

The same shift that occurs at the school site must also occur in some fashion in the classroom setting as well. The teacher must somehow create a situation where the learner can understand the goals enough to set indicators, a process of measurement and decisions of pace. "Here we are in Chemistry 2. It's hard, but interesting I think. Let me spend some time describing the material and the difficult transitions."   After that he might ask these questions of the class:

How fast do you want to go?

How do you want to assess yourselves?

What responsibility do you have to and for each other in terms of mastering the materials?

What he is doing is passing on to them in a formal and visible way, responsibility for setting indicators, measurement, and pace. And he is calling the question of individual learner and the community of learners. The subtext of this dialogue has to continue through the entire treatment of Chemistry 2. "I am not responsible for your learning. I already know it. I'll help every way I can. But it is *your* issue and challenge. Yours individually *and* together."

As the focus of education shifts from teaching to learning and from ranking to individual growth, the entire tone of the process changes as well. It can become for these young people a deeply positive experience, building up their sense of their own strengths and capacities, and worth.

This is the real reason why restructuring is the key to quality in education. The environment for both teacher and learner is the same -- a classroom, a school. If we can change life for the teacher -- granting empowerment, encouraging ownership and caring, and redirecting responsibility -- we can change life for the learner.

Chapter Eleven: The System As Learner - The Oversite Committee

We have reached a point in our journey where it is time for a second metaphor. In the beginning, while we were still developing a strategy, we thought in terms of a living organism in a Steady State of powerful equilibrium. That metaphor implied change as a systemic challenge, and an integrated, total strategy.

We now are ready to think about implementing that strategy, to think about how to unstick the Steady State. Here, the metaphor is that of a building, a structure. It is basically a sound structure, but there are parts of it you don't like. You want to change some of the building's features, but you don't want to tear it down in the process.

So you build a scaffold to work on a building that is still occupied. Life goes on inside while you are hammering away. Then one day the scaffold comes down, and when it does, the old building should look very different. It should be better integrated. Deeply empowered at the point of delivery. The customer should have a strong powerful voice, and the top should be in the habit of listening and learning constantly. It will be the old building but all the features that didn't work are transformed.

Our strategy for change is site-based decision making. It is, unquestionably, a *structural* intervention. We know what aspects of the old building we want to change, where we have to place our scaffold, and how the different sections of the scaffold must be joined. Above all, we know that this set of scaffolds must be strong enough so that from it we can create pressure on the underlying structure, enough pressure that it will dislodge the Steady State and realign the old System.

The first place to build a scaffold is at Boundary One, with the anchors of the system: the board, the management, and the union leadership. Here, the aspects of the structure we are trying to change appear as three distinct pathologies.

1. ***The lack of horizontal integration between the three anchors***. They don't really know how to talk openly to each other, much less how to listen to one another. They most often come together in a wary dance of mutual mistrust, stepping to different beats. The scaffold you erect against this pathology must give them a place where they can safely work together toward their common goals, and listen to and respect one another's view and data.

2. ***The non-listening system***. Not only do the three anchors have trouble listening to one another, they have cut themselves off from the system's bottom-up data. Yet without that data, the anchors will never understand the general patterns of blockages, and be able to work on problem-solving to unstick the overall system. There has to be some way for the anchors at the district level to learn from the process of change occurring at the various sites and classroom levels, while continuing their own improvement.

3. ***The vertical drop***. This is the problem of the hierarchy itself, and the difficulty of getting good, straight information constantly flowing up and down the hierarchy. It is closely related to the lack of bottom-up data, but the pathology is more one of lack of trust than of non-listening.

    You build a scaffold against these three pathologies by creating a place where the system can learn to do things differently. This is an intervention that creates a place, *even when it is not natural*, where the anchors can do deep collaborative listening, deep integration, and deep learning about the place they own together.   This temporary structure is the District Oversite Committee.

"There has to be some way for the anchors...to learn from the process of change...while continuing their own improvement."

The Oversite Committee is the place where the system *as a system* can stop, look at itself, and work on healing itself. The union, or the management, or the board, can each do it for themselves individually, but without an Oversite Committee there is nowhere that the system as a whole can learn. Each one of the groups knows where its strengths and some of its own shortfalls are. It needs to find out what the other groups know.

The Oversite Committee is also the place where the learning from the individual sites is integrated. Without it school-focused restructuring is a series of pilot programs: isolated successes perhaps, but no systemic movement.

GIVING PERMISSION

The first task of the Oversite Committee is to grant permission. In the process of educating themselves about school restructuring, the anchors can begin to talk openly about the possible blockages to success. The larger system will witness the process, and begin to get the message that the three anchors are serious about this. When all three are finally committed, each of them should give *formal* permission in a very public way.

**"The larger system will witness the process, and begin
to get the message that the three anchors are serious about this."**

The school board, after sufficient orientation of the community, should enter into an official policy of the board supporting the restructuring and decentralizing of decision-making. The union and management should, ideally, add some sort of letter of agreement to the contract, subject to renewal at each negotiation. This letter, as we have noted earlier, should not be a lengthy document, but it should clearly say that both union and management are entering into a process of change together aimed at decentralization and empowerment at the site level. It can include a paragraph about a collaborative approach to finding the time and money to do the process. It should surely include the possibility for waivers from policy, school regulations, and union contract when the appropriate anchor group has given permission. (Appendix A)

SETTING PARAMETERS

Having given permission, the Oversite Committee now needs to take a second step that is almost the polar opposite: to establish limits.   The anchors must set clear parameters, and publish them openly.   Nobody gets to operate in any system as if there were no parameters, so why not say what they are?

The system is owed a statement of *what it is you are asking them to get into*, and *what it is you are uncomfortable with them getting into* at this point. Without these parameters, nothing will move, because everyone will feel it is a trap.

The parameters can be framed as a sort of invitation that says, "*Push* us on this. Make us change these parameters when you feel the time is right. We expect you to move; you can expect us to move as well." If the first permission-giving was done well, then the setting of parameters is in some senses an even stronger message that restructuring is more than rhetoric.

MAKING DECISIONS DIFFERENTLY

For the first two years or so, the parameters are helpful as a means to begin to feel your way into various areas carefully and well. The early discussion around this issue focuses on questions of power and absolute decision-making control: "Either *we* make the decision, or *they* do." This is the point to begin a discussion of the continuum of decision-making that actually exists in real educational systems.

There is an entire spectrum of decisions being made every day, in every classroom, school, and district. What are we going to teach? Who is going to teach it? How do we evaluate? How do we organize to teach it? What are our resources? When do we begin and end the day? What logistics need to be in place?

Some of those decisions have already been made. Federal law, state legislation, and national tests are givens. There's no pushing those parameters.

Other decisions can be claimed with great legitimacy by one or other of the district actors.   "This is mine. But I will keep you informed about the direction of my decisions."   The union, for example, has certain rights under the contract that give it decision making authority in areas like seniority or due process.

Still other decisions can be made in a more consultative fashion: "This is mine. But I will discuss it with you, and I would like your input." An example of this would be personnel choices, scheduling, or evaluation procedures.

Further along the spectrum comes a point at which you say, "This is *ours*. This decision is going to be made jointly. The principal and the staff (or the anchors and the site) will work it out."   This venue of collaborative decisions is broad and destined to grow. It is precisely this broad range that mitigates the either/or from the pure power language of absolute decision-making control.

Further along is the position that says "This decision is yours. I would like to have some influence on it, but clearly, I understand you make the final decision." Parents or students could surely talk to the teaching staff about discipline policy in this fashion.

Finally, there is the position that says "I understand this is your decision. When you have made it, let me know."

The process of restructuring involves changing where along that spectrum the decisions of who? what? and how? are made. The questions you keep asking are "What do you hold?" "What do you let go?" You can create a matrix that lists the types of decisions on one axis and the gamut of control and decentralization at the other axis. The four or five main categories around decision-making probably would be the curricular and the educational decisions, the personnel and staffing decisions, the financial decisions, and finally the logistical ones. One of the early learning exercises, in fact, is when the Oversite Committee begins to map the system's profile and hear the differences of opinion as to where decision-making actually rests at this moment.

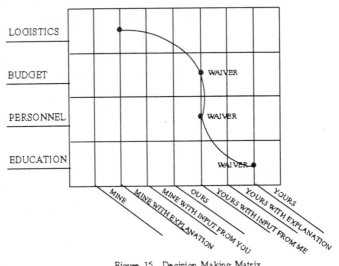

Figure 15. Decision Making Matrix

This is the moment too, when the Oversite Committee can choose to focus on a specific area. For instance, some choose curricular issues for the first years and deliberately try to decentralize these issues. They soon discover that whereas there is considerable latitude in the early grades, by the high school years there is a certain amount of outside control of one type or another, requirements that force the curriculum into certain kinds of concentrations, or even delineating very specifically the content of advanced placement courses.

This type of discussion around the matrix helps curtail much of the early either/or rhetoric around who has decision-making authority. The Oversite group very clearly says "This is how it looks to us. These decisions are going to be made here. These decisions should be made here. And these decisions can be made here." In the beginning, a preponderance of the important decisions are found to be centralized, and it is difficult for the anchors to see what they can safely relinquish. Over time the anchors accept a general rule of thumb that as many decisions should be made at the point of delivery as they can tolerate. Then the oversite group can say to the sites: "Insofar as you need parts of other pieces to make your teaching and learning more effective, come back to us." This invitation is where the system begins to grow and learn. It also creates some interesting tensions.

Let's say the teachers and management at SITE A have really pulled together. They decide they want to create a certain kind of learning environment, and then do so. Three years later, three key positions in the school have opened up. Someone has retired, another person's spouse has transferred out of state, a staff member has been promoted.

Under the old model, the anchors would move in at this point. The union would say, "We have a seniority list here." Management would say, "We need to develop a skill profile and fill the positions according to that." In this way, two of the three anchors would fill the school's slots.

"This is the moment that creates the tension to torque the system."

But over at SITE A, these people now own the thing they have created. *They* want to control their teacher selection to their team. When the anchors say, "We are going to make those decisions in the usual way," the group comes right back and says, "We've created a special context here, and it requires a certain comfort with this type of discipline and instruction. Those are the criteria to use, and we need people who are excited to be part of that type of place."

This is the moment that creates the tension to torque the system. The site is going to take the position that "We can't hold what it is we have built *here* if you won't let us have input over *there*." And it will say to the union and the management "You created us. It is up to you to find ways to let us keep going." At that point, if the anchors truly understand their role, the parameters will move, and the restructuring will break through to a higher level.

If it is a real learning system, the overall system as it struggles will tell you where to put decisions. The act of setting parameters is simply creating a benchmark that says, "This is where we have begun."

FINDING RESOURCES

The next major issue for the Oversite Committee, once it has set parameters and given permission, is to begin to look for the resources that will be needed. The time, the money, and the training necessary for the process will be significant.

There are at least two very different kinds of training requirements. The first is the early requirement to help the Site Councils (and any other teams) acquire the process skills necessary to do this kind of work. Some team building, process training and problem solving models are enormously helpful early on.

These skills in the "process" of group work are critical to the quality and speed of the early phases of restructuring. A lot of behavior change is called for in the early days. This is the "how" of change.

A second set of skills is needed as well, even at the beginning. Enrichment of content ideas such as changes in curriculum, approaches to learning itself, motivational theory and so on, must be made available to the sites. Much of this skill has traditionally been located in supervisory roles away from the schools and classroom. It should now be repositioned in a consultative way so that the decision-making configurations can be exposed to good action-research educational examples and the best thinking in the country as it touches their issues. Much of what was previously captured in Boundary Five at the Central Office should now be redistributed to enrich the problem-solving in the sites and in the ad hoc teams.

As the Oversite Committee contemplates the resources needed and the resources available, it will need to allow the launches of the school sites in some staggered fashion. Very few systems are able to move overnight to system-wide site councils and problem-solving units. This logistical responsibility ensures that the quality of support will be there as needed over the first few years.

FINDING TIME

Finally, there is perhaps the most difficult issue of all, and that is the issue of time. If there is a single characteristic difference between the old Steady State and the emerging new learning system, it is the definition of work. The old Steady State system views thinking time as non-productive time. In effect, it is saying that teaching (or assembling a car, or pouring steel) is *non-thinking* work. Thinking is something you should be doing on your own time. When teachers asked for more thinking time, the old Steady State would say, "Can't spare the time out of the classroom."

"And the answer in 1975 essentially was, 'They are too busy doing it wrong to figure out how to do it right.' That's where we are with much of the educational system."

It's as though you went into a Ford factory in 1975 and said, "You have got 2,000 guys in here and you need them to help you think about how to build better cars." And the answer would be, "No time. They are too busy building cars." And you'd say, "That is the problem! The car is junk! The reason it's junk is that your people aren't helping you build it better." And the answer in 1975 essentially was, "They are too busy doing it wrong to figure out how to do it right." That's where we are with much of the educational system.

There are about four possible responses to this problem of getting enough time to think. For teachers the common response has been to volunteer their time. They would finish up their teaching and planning and monitoring and grading hours and then they would come in after school to work, unpaid, on site councils and problem-solving committees. They did it because they cared enormously. But you wouldn't go into a steel mill and say, "We are not making very good steel. The competition is sneaking up on us. Could some of you guys please stay over and help us figure out how to make better steel?" You wouldn't do that; the workplace would explode. But for some reason we expect teachers to do that.

One of the reasons they do it is that the alternative is just as unattractive. That is what I would call the General Motors model. When General Motors finally decided to involve workers in problem-solving groups, they couldn't just shut down the line. So they took thirty highly skilled workers and assigned them to "float" all day long. You could pull twelve people off the assembly line to problem-solve for an hour or so, and insert twelve of these floaters to do their jobs.

Teachers have an equivalent to these floaters. They call them subs. The problem is that subs don't work out very well. First of all, it's tough to hold the quality of instruction with substitute teachers. But even more significant, there is the fact that it takes almost as much time to prepare a sub as to do the thing yourself. It's just not worth the effort, so some teachers swallow hard, teach the day's classes, and then drag in to the evening site council meeting. It's fine, if you don't want a personal life.

A third approach is the Ford solution. About 1981 Ford built into its contract with the UAW a provision that the company would pay straight time for extra hours every other week that workers could spend on problem solving above and beyond their regular work. They were in effect saying, "We will pay you to spend extra time thinking." Some school Site Councils have adopted that model, treating the thinking time as additional work above the teaching load, to be paid for as additional work.

This is an improvement over the first two models, but it is still based on a crazy distinction that we have made in this country between thinking and doing. The Japanese have demonstrated to us the absurdity of that dichotomy.

At Toyota, they have structured their system so that every man and woman gets paid on the basis of a full work week, but only 90 percent of that time is spent actually building cars. The other 10 percent is scheduled for problem-solving or training time or communication meetings.

You would think that this would put Toyota at a productivity disadvantage, since they have 10 percent fewer hours to spend working at building cars. But when you lay it out statistically, and follow it for a few years, you find something absolutely amazing. The plant starts out at a 10 percent productivity disadvantage compared with its American counterparts. By the third year, its output equals that of a normal Big Three factory. By the fifth year, they have passed the Detroit norm, and are operating at 100 percent of the plant's rated capacity. But the truly amazing thing happens around the seventh year. By the seventh year, that Toyota plant is operating at about 115 to 120 percent of its rated capacity...because they have been redesigning the factory and the equipment as they went along, constantly improving so that it could produce more cars, more efficiently, with higher quality.

> **"...you will find that if you are willing to put time into doing things better what happens is that it gets better forever."**

Time after time in places where it has been tried, you will find that if you are willing to put time into doing things better what happens is that it gets better *forever*. Whereas if you achieve a certain level and stop there, and try to hold it there, you run into the law of entropy, leading to certain decline. This is the real disadvantage we're working under, and it has been proven over and over again.

Somebody has got to say to the community, to the parents, to the state legislature "In order to teach your children better, we have got to teach them *less*. We need to have time to figure out how to do it better, how to improve. We need time to sit down with you, to sit down with each other, with children, to find out what's working and what isn't, to figure out how to do it better." Good teachers understand that they don't have to be standing there teaching all the time. That takes away the children's chance to learn. Learning does not stop when one is not teaching. The old definition of "contact hours" sounds more like guard duty or baby-sitting, rather than teaching.

Instead, in a truly bizarre twist, we have taken the old factory model and applied it to education. We negotiated it into our contracts, defining what a teacher does in these "contact hours." Having done that, we are looking to the Ford and GM models for our examples of how to change it. Ford and GM are slowly learning to wean themselves from that thinking, but it is alive and well in public education.

Somehow, as it looks at what it will take to change its schools, the Oversite Committee will need to find the courage and the commitment to say, "We will find the time for teachers to spend doing this reflective work." By the third or fourth year, there should be a policy and implementation plan that allows a significant number of men and women in the system to take as much as three or four hours every two weeks for reflection.

It will take courage because, for the community at large, quality improvement often translates into increasing "contact days" in the classroom. Somehow the community must be educated to the need for increased time for thinking, planning, communication and problem-solving. It is amazing how the parents respond when they understand what is at stake. At the middle school in Central Kitsap, Washington, the Site Council went to the parents with a proposal for extra thinking and problem-solving time, and the parents came back to them with an even better way of going about it. Rather than early release every other Wednesday, the parents suggested starting school two hours later. "We didn't want them all over the community on Wednesday afternoons, but we knew where they'd be early on Wednesday mornings if we let them sleep late."

This is still within the normal frame of reference for the members of the Oversite Committee. Most anchors are comfortable giving permission, setting parameters, finding resources. That is, after all, what anchors are suppose to do in a traditional top/down Steady State.

LISTENING AND LEARNING

The final and most important of the Oversite Committee's activities is more difficult for the anchors. This is where the commitment is truly tested. This final, most important activity is to *listen*, to create a place where the three principal groups - the Board, the management, and union leadership - can come together and talk in a non-threatening exchange about the place they own together.

This is where the system can do deep collaborative work, where it can look at itself as a system. This is where the system learns. Strategically, that is what this whole intervention is all about. For deep, long- lasting change, you need a place where the oversite anchors can come together regularly and talk about what is working and not working, listen to representatives of the Site Councils, and see their own anchor functions as blocking or enabling.

"They are asking the sites to problem-solve their shortfall with them in a culture that is afraid to talk about shortfalls."

This process is not easy for any of the players. The beginning is messy. It is hard for the anchors to have to sit in meetings for a long time, listening to each other and the sites. It is tedious. There are moments when the anchors will say,"What are we doing here?"

Coming out of a Steady State, the anchors will typically say to the Site Councils "You have three hours to tell us how you are doing." And, the Site Councils, with their own Steady State histories, say to themselves, "Oh oh! We had better not tell them how slow it is or they will pull the plug." So they put on a dog and pony show and basically don't tell the anchors anything.

So the anchors have to get smart and say, "You have got twenty minutes to tell us how well you are doing. Then you must spend an hour telling us where you are stuck; where it is you are struggling; where we are in the way; what you are learning." They are asking the sites to problem-solve their shortfall with them in a culture that is afraid to talk about shortfalls.

At first, no one will believe they mean it. But somewhere along the line, a principal, staff, and parents will say to each other: "Let's go in and test it." Then they actually walk in and tell the truth. The whole system watches to see what happens. If that Oversite Committee starts asking good questions, the rest of the system will say, "Maybe they really want to hear it." And, from that moment on, the system can break through to a new level of trust and learning.

It will take constant repetition and reinforcement to prove that the hierarchy is actually trying to learn and help, rather than punish for negative data, before this system begins openly and honestly to talk about it strengths and weaknesses. But once listening and learning really begins to happen, it will allow the system to transform itself. The Oversite Committee will work on the areas where it blocks and does not listen, and open itself up to the information from the customer, from the teachers, from the support staff and from the students.

Along the way, the anchors themselves can be transformed. Gradually, they will seek fundamental changes in the way each of them exercises responsibility. Typically, in the old system, each of them holds vehemently to past victories, and to past rights, as if changing them would somehow diminish their power and presence. In this safe place created by the scaffold, the anchors themselves will learn how to give and take with one another and constantly reconfigure and restructure to find the best solutions for the system at this moment. In the process, each of them will find the energy, the creativity, and the understanding to carry out their moral and legal responsibilities at a higher level.

Chapter Twelve: The School As Learner - The Site Council

The Oversite Committee is the first structural intervention that may resist change. It is politically hard, takes time, and does not reach directly to the site. However, one must create a place where a non-integrated, non-listening system can begin to heal itself, and allow the first steps to be taken at the various sites.

At the sites, we need a somewhat different structure, a scaffold designed to "hold" principal, staff and parents in tension against the old Steady State. It is deliberately built to bring pressure on the three main dysfunctions usually found in a school in the old structure:

1.   The vertical drop that divides the principal and teachers in a hierarchy marked by some fear and distrust - (and teacher to student as well.)

2.   The lack of horizontal integration in the school, department to department, class to class, teacher to teacher. (student to student)

3.   The resistance of the system to its main customer, the parent.

The scaffold we build here is the site council. Coming out of the old Steady State, there is usually enormous confusion about what a site council is meant to be and to do. "Empowerment" becomes a shorthand for transferring control from one locus to another. The whole intervention becomes a power issue, and it bogs down there without ever having the opportunity to budge the system.

PUTTING TORQUE ON THE SYSTEM

It's important, therefore, to spell out exactly what a site council is, and what it isn't. It will take some time before the real function of the site council is understood, but from the very start one at least needs to confront some major misconceptions.

This is *not*, first of all, a permanent structure. You are not creating a new structural "answer," a Steady State Two, that replaces the old model. This is a temporary scaffold, and it will be taken down when the system has changed and it is no longer needed. It is a transitional moment, a place where various actors can behave in significantly different ways without having to deny all their old data and experience and responsibilities in Steady State One.

Second, it is *not* primarily a decision-making mechanism. This is not principalship by committee. A Site Council that focuses only on decision-making tends to make the intervention solely a power issue. It often exhausts itself on petty issues and control struggles and never gets on to the main business, which is *driving* the change. It never moves on to unstick the school, and its relationships, and never gets down to its real job. A Site Council is put in place to push its own site, and as a result to push the larger system, to push the anchors, and the customer and community to look at fundamental issues of the school structure and delivery. *Site Councils are there to create torque on the system, to create such tension that the system must unstick.*

This may seem like a contradiction, because if it is not a new governance structure, then what is its role in decision-making?

The answer is that this is the place that can and should audit *all* decision-making at the site, saying to the principal, "Did you talk to the right people?" "Have you considered this?" "Are you sure this is the right decision?" And, eventually saying, "Should you be making this decision or should someone else?" It can say to a faculty "Should you be taking responsibility for assessment, better linkage to parents?" Or to students, "Is this behavior issue your responsibility?"

The Site Council is, above all, a learning structure. Its job is to keep dreaming the school, inventing it, driving the change, and learning from it. It makes sure that everything that happens is done in a more collaborative fashion with deeper listening, in better contact with the customer, and with greater responsibility at the lower levels. It keeps driving, unsticking, and moving sites along through empowerment shifts. At every point it asks "Where is the appropriate place for this decision to be made?" "With whom?" "In what configuration?"

A good Site Council knows that every decision has an appropriate place in the spectrum of authority, and is willing to test that venue constantly. Again and again it asks, "Have we included all the necessary actors?" "Have we listened well?" "Is this working?"

The Site Council should not be confused with a legislature. The old Steady State equated number of seats with voting power, and this leads to some very volatile early discussions on Site Council composition.

One reflexive response is to say "We will structure a Site Council to address this specific dysfunction." So, if the perceived problem is a bad relationship between customer and school, you simply create a 50/50 structure of parents and teachers, and end up with a powerless principal. Or if it seems that the issue is the relationship between management and union, you structure a site council of, on the one hand, teachers and support staff (duly elected), and on the other hand, principal and administrators. In either case you have just replaced one hierarchy with another, or substituted a simplistic realignment of roles for a part of the Steady State. This type of "change" misses the central point of restructuring.

On the other hand, this cannot be simply a structure that makes recommendations and hopes that something will happen. It needs to have power and responsibility and authority in certain areas. It must be powerful enough to make decisions where appropriate.

STAFFING THE SITE COUNCIL

Clearly, the principal needs to be part of the new structure. Alongside the principal, the majority of the actors need to be the professional educators, since they are directly involved in what the work is all about. Support staff should have a voice, and in high schools, students should be present as well, although this is not the primary place where they will have a chance for input and activity.
Finally, if the Site Council is truly to be a problem solving entity, it must obviously include a voice from the customer - the parents and the community - as well.

If you intend your site council to be a functioning problem-solving group, the ideal size is somewhere between ten and fifteen members. Anything larger than fifteen becomes merely a communication structure, not a problem-solving unit, and anything smaller than six or seven is probably not large enough to capture the complexity of a site. A good problem solving Site Council would include the principal, five or six teachers at various grade levels, two or three support staff, three or four from the parent group and the community, and in high school, one or two students.

Generally, a group like this lacks the skills to work effectively at the beginning, and a certain amount of training and other support is needed from the system itself, such as:

1.   You will need to *teach group problem-solving skills and consensual decision-making* with enough depth so that all the participants have built up their skills and experience in this area. This requires early training, and then ongoing reemphasis.

2.   Given the background of the system and the fact that you are also asking the customer to be involved actively, you need *the ability to deal with some early conflict*, since the several worlds will not come together easily and quickly.

3.   Apart from these process skills of problem-solving and conflict resolution, over the long haul you will need to *make content expertise accessible at the site level*. As more and more of the teaching decisions are made on the site, much of the expertise in curricular and other specialized areas should become available at the point of delivery, as a consultative and enriching presence.

Slowly, with help, the group learns how to move as a group, having heard all of its voices. They learn that the process is not a model to achieve unanimity, nor is it a model for pure voting. It is a process that is often called "consensus" and it really is a way to hear, very carefully, differing points of view before the group can move ahead. The minority positions have to learn how to make their positions clear, and at a certain point, having been heard fairly, they must learn to move with the group toward some solution. It is a process of thoughtfulness and listening in which all of the members ordinarily have to give up some portion of their opinion in order to reach agreement.

Early-on it takes a lot of doing. Since each of the major actors in polarized systems comes from a deep history of position-taking, and intransigence as the way to gain power and to influence events; consensus sounds soft or unreal, and in the old model it probably was. But slowly, over time, as the group begins to problem-solve successfully, the power and legitimacy of the consensus model grows in mutual interests and respect for one another.

It's slow, hard work and you need to think of it in terms of years, not months. The first year will probably be spent going through some fairly fundamental exercises that will build a deep base for longer term change. Some events of this first year would include:

1. *Team building* with the new configuration, which would include discussions of what this new structure is all about, how the team will work, how often it will meet, what its decision making process ought to be, how far its authority will extend, and how it will communicate to the rest of the system.

2.   *A small diagnostic event* of its own, more
        qualitative than a strict survey, to take the pulse of
        the school, and include a sampling of parental
        attitudes (and students' where appropriate) and those
        of other community leaders.   One of the early,
        difficult decisions will be whether to make the
        findings public.   Since they are usually fairly
        negative, this decision takes a certain amount of
        courage coming out of the traditional Steady State
        model, but it is an absolutely critical one.

3.   A *plan for experimentation*, change, and
        improvement should be developed out of the team
        building and the findings of the diagnosis, and then
        published.

EVALUATING PROGRESS - INDICATORS AND MEASUREMENTS

At the beginning of the second year, the Site
Council can flesh out the plan, identifying some internal
quantitative measures they believe in, adding some key
district measures from the district's to their own qualitative
measurements, and begin to build their own learning and
self auditing processes. They should bring each year to
completion with a retreat, reviewing the plan, goals, and
measurement devices, evaluating themselves, and publishing
the results as their own report card. This report card,over
time, will result in a growing clarity of goals and how they
will be measured, and eventually lead to the emergence of
a culture of constant learning and improvement.

A report card for a middle school might look like this: "Here are our Iowa Tests of Basic Skills (ITBS) scores. We did well in this area, making good progress over last year, but we still need to improve in several other areas. Here is our strategy for improvement..."

"In addition, we had decided as a school and community that when your children come here as 6th Graders they would begin to learn other things, and we would spend the next three years teaching them those additional qualitative skills."

- "We decided to teach them how to collaborate, how to work together in teams."

- "We decided to teach them to be self-empowered learners, capable of going off and working on their own projects without being forced."

- "We also decided to build in a service component - service to the community and particularly to our elderly. We decided to develop courses in this, cognitive as well as practical. Here are some of our successes and some of our shortfalls to-date."

- "We are now developing ways to measure our success in these qualitative learnings. We need your help in doing that."

Notice that this type of report card does not emphasize rankings. It talks in terms of specific values embodied in this particular school's curriculum - not compared to any other school's teaching but rooted in its own mission, goals, and performance.

Every site starts from a different position in the Steady State. Some are more ready than others, for example, to take the risks of publicly owning some negative information about themselves and their organization. The process can only move forward as quickly as the organization is capable of supporting it at that moment. Off-the-shelf solutions and lock-step training just don't further the process, and they waste time, money and good will.

Even so, there must be some visible progress. If the process doesn't lead to something of substance by the third year, then key actors inside and out will begin to fall away. If the Site Council gets stuck in endless process, or simple "governance" debates, and doesn't get into significant teaching-learning issues by the second year, it becomes suspect and vulnerable. It must at least show the promise of significant curricular and classroom reform as the third year begins. Sometimes you just can't wait until conditions are perfect before you take the high dive. The greatest danger is to lose the opportunity.

TURNING THE TIDE - BUILDING ENERGY FOR CHANGE

The dynamics of the momentum follow a fairly predictable pattern. When first beginning a change process within a site, about one-fourth of the people will come along with you. But that doesn't mean a thing, because those people have *always* been with you. They have just been doing this thing *sub rosa*. They are wonderful, caring, committed folks, but their support isn't going to move the system. They don't have the rest of the world with them.

There is another 10 percent *against* this process from the beginning as they are against almost all change efforts or initiatives of any kind. Sometimes we fool ourselves that the supportive 20 percent, or the negative 10 percent speak for the system. They don't.

The key moment comes when you begin to touch the middle group. Those people have been around for a while, and they know how the world works, and they are skeptical.

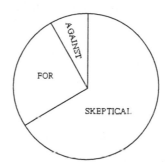

Figure 16. Distribution of Interest, Support & Energy for School Change Process

They will keep their heads down, and they won't come along until something has happened to convince them that this time it is going to be different. Until you hook the cautious 70 percent nothing has really changed. But once they begin to move, the tide turns, and you can begin truly to change the context of the school.

The Site Council is the key structure, but it must be used correctly. If one only focuses at the site and tries to run a school with it, it will falter and fall. It can be a powerful change mechanism that can drive the deep shifts at the site, pressure the total system, and build a learning system as it goes.

It follows then that the real key is a number of these Site Councils moving in tandem. The pressure for a single right way, or pilot site diffuses into experimentation, variety, learning, and expansion of horizons.   Second, the cumulative power of many Site Councils on a district system will make it impossible to maintain old models, and support the new one emerging, and the system will per force have to restructure itself.

Chapter Thirteen: Teacher and Student As Workers

The real work of schools is learning. That is the coal to be dug, and every other role somehow has to connect to that work, support it, enrich it, try to improve it.

Starting with learning, instead of with teaching, a school ends up shifting some fundamental frames for all the actors. Suddenly, the student is no longer at the end of the long chain of command/control. You walk away from the military model with its spear carriers at the bottom having no responsibility except to follow orders. Instead you say to each of these student workers "This is *your endeavor*. It is up to you. How do you plan to succeed at it?"

141

Yes, the student/learner still needs support and help in understanding the issues and the seriousness of the undertaking. Yes, these are still children, and like all children, they need guidance. There isn't a teacher in the country who doesn't feel that tug.

But within this desire to support and guide lies the constant temptation to go further, to *see that the work gets done;* in short, to take on responsibility for its performance. Too often, this shift of responsibility creates first dependency, then a disconnect, then control on one side, and passive/aggressive anger and apathy on the other.

It becomes "us against them," and since "they" hold the cards for now, the choice for many is to fold or to cheat. Do those kids end up reacting any differently than the young autoworkers who made life miserable for GM in the 1970s? Someone above has set the goals, defined the tasks, established the measurement and tried to enforce it. In the school this comes out of caring, to be sure. But the result is the same.

When those who do the work experience their work as someone else's problem, so that the system tells them every which way that their role is not the important one, then the quality and attention of the work, the worker, and the work place disappear.

BUILDING RESPONSIBILITY

When I first began consulting in schools, I visited a high school in Seattle. I had just come out of a tough week interviewing steelworkers in Gary, Indiana, and I was ready for a change. For several days, I watched a group of five boys horsing around in classrooms and the cafeteria. They were full of life and it was nice to see their energy and spirit. But the more I watched them, the more familiar it looked. Finally, all I could see was a group of forty-year-old steelworkers in Gary. All their joy came out of defeating the system. It was their life's work. And, of course, in sabotaging the system, what they couldn't see was that they were sabotaging themselves.

> "When those who do the work experience their work as someone else's problem, so that the system tells them every which way that their role is not the important one, then the quality and attention of the work, the worker, and the workplace disappear."

You can't be responsible for someone else's work; you can only be responsible for creating a setting that lets him or her be responsible. American industry has learned that lesson, painfully, over the last ten years. But this language is politically dangerous in education now, since it can be twisted to sound like one doesn't care about children. It is, however, too controlling over protective approaches that fail in respect for the child, the learner, the other person. (NOTE: Peter Block's new book *Stewardship*, 1993, Barrett-Koehler, presents a wonderful discussion of this issue, conceptually and concretely.)

In training a good young competitive athlete, a coach wouldn't say "I'm working with you so that you can run a 4:30 mile. That is good enough to qualify for the state championships." Instead, you would concentrate on creating an inner drive that makes her keep on moving the marker every time she achieves a goal. She wouldn't ease up on practice just because she had broken 4:25. She'd start driving for 4:20, and then 4:15, and see just how far she could push it. So long as she is driving herself, the joy will keep her going. *It is the challenge of responsibility in the learner that has to drive the process.*

If you start with the learning instead of the teaching, it forces a change in the role of the teacher. Now the task is as enabler, not controller.

GIVING UP DEPENDENCY

Here is how it might look. It is the first day of the school year and you walk into Latin 202. You say "Ladies, gentlemen, lovely to have you here. This is hard work, but you have chosen to do it and it's a wonderful choice. I am glad I'm along with you. Let's talk about what the world says Latin 202 is."

Here is their connection to Boundary Four - Information Systems. Boundary Four was set as a series of goals and indicators by the board, then refined and made specific to the school's special learning environment by the Site Council. Now students and teacher, within those larger contexts, begin to establish the concrete goals and measurements for themselves.

You, the teacher in this classroom, are now going to ask this group of fifteen and sixteen-year-olds how they want to take responsibility for setting and achieving these goals and standards for Latin 202. You say, "Okay, we have 35 weeks together. How do you want to proceed with this material? I have a couple of ideas, but it is up to you. You should know that there is a really tough section about a third of the way through and then another difficult piece about two-thirds through when we get to the subjunctive and optative. We will probably need a little more time there. But, how we handle the pace is your decision."

You talk about that for a while and then say, ""Now how do you want to *assess yourselves?*" The kids say "But that's your problem." You say, "No, my problem is to make sure we *have* some assessment. *How* we do it is up to you. There are about three or four ways to go about it, and we need to talk about it."

They may decide to have a regularly scheduled quiz every Friday. You then say, "What responsibility do you want to take for each other? If four or five of you get D's on the quiz, for instance, do you as a class want to pull back and wait for them, help them?"

"You can't be responsible for someone else's work; you can only be responsible for creating a setting that lets him or her be responsible."

In this way, you have laid out the system's goals for them, but then engaged them in deciding their own goals, pace, assessment techniques, and their degree of common responsibility. What you are saying to them at every point is that achieving the goals and standards is *their* responsibility. You are simply there to enable it. To do this in the early grades is just as critical. Interestingly, we know and practice this approach with respect to behavior, but much less so in learning.

"No teaching activity should end up creating dependency or taking responsibility away from the student."

It is true that certain pieces of a high school education are less negotiable than others. Some of the hard sciences, like calculus, are probably best taught when a teacher transmits his or her knowledge directly to the student, saying "I have this. You need it from me. Here it is." But, in most other areas, there are opportunities to shift that burden of responsibility in a way that allows the students to truly own it.

No teaching activity should end up creating dependency or taking responsibility away from the student. Nor should administration, or parenting, or measurement. Beginning with this principle, we move "up the line," redefining roles all along the way.

For the teacher, finally, the shift means getting out of the hated role of enforcer. Most teachers go into the profession because they naturally have powerful empathy and listening skills. Now, at last, the system gives the teacher permission to use them.

It goes even further. The new system says, "We never let you stretch those muscles in the past. If they have atrophied, or if your past experience in the old system burned you, we will help you restore yourself. We all need to rediscover our ability to listen deeply, to reflect constantly on how well our teaching is working. Let us give each other feedback, and we will learn as we go along. And, by the way, let's create the same learning environment for our children."

This, of course, requires a change in the entire assessment system. In most schools today, the principal observes a teacher's performance twice a year and writes up an evaluation. The process doesn't sort out anything, because the principal doesn't really know from that brief encounter, what is going on.

In a healthy environment, the teacher would say to her peers "I need three or four of you to observe me at least nine times this semester. The part I think I really need help on is getting the kids to ask questions as we go along. I don't feel comfortable doing this just yet and I know you do it much better." That teacher knows the weakness she wants to work on, and she is comfortable having peers in there helping her do it. She is in charge of her own learning and improvement and her own evaluation.

That is so very different from a top/down approach where the principal has the responsibility and the whole thing smacks of danger. In that kind of environment the teacher would never take a risk, never ask someone to observe her in her weakness so that she could get help. Instead, when the principal comes into the classroom, the teachers think "Oh oh! Here she is. I'll go to my strength." The result is that too few ever learn.

To come to this moment when the assessment can lead to learning and the goal is always improvement, the anchors will have to move, as well. The union and the management will have to rethink the way they handle negative data and both the individual's and the system's rights and responsibilities. Under the old system, if feedback about a given teacher's performance is negative, the union's role would be to move in, readying the defense, summoning up all the protections it can muster.

Management does it partly to squelch feedback by adopting a punitive and legalistic response. It is the old enforcer's voice saying, "Quality, or else!" How can a teaching staff possibly work on quality when the data that points the way to improvement is hushed up? This is one of the toughest issues the union and management will grapple with, but sooner or later it has to move.

THINKING TIME AND DOING TIME

By comparison, the issue of time is a piece of cake. In the old Steady State, the system is full of assigned tasks and careful scheduling and control, and minute contract language. The underlying assumption is that the system has been thought out and perfected to the best possible level, and everyone's task is simply to maintain it. So the traditional dance between union and management is that management sets those goals and measurements and assigned tasks, while the union makes sure that people are not abused by them.

The problem is that everyone buys into the stable state on which the roles have been assigned and contracts negotiated. The thing almost by definition can never get better, and that means that probably over time its only direction is to get a little worse.

It is a crazy, backward system built on time management, on the theory that productivity is filling time with activity. There is almost no time for reflection, no time for quality improvement, no time for listening to yourself and the other teachers in a reflective fashion that brings true learning. As long as "thinking time" is designed in opposition to and borrowed from "doing time" you have not designed the future. The definition of the role of the teacher and the student has to include not only doing, but also thinking about how to do it better. And that definition will reach into the design of the job, the time that is allocated, and the pay that is given in response to both activities.

Responsibility, support, reflective time, and learning have got to define a "place" whose main activity is growth and learning, and the term "learner" describes everyone's role - principal, teacher, support staff, and student - even parents in the process.

Chapter Fourteen:
Parents and
Community -
The Customer
As Energy and
Resource

      How on earth are you going to get the community with you? How can you hook this customer who is indifferent or opposed to you to begin with, doesn't believe what you say because he feels you have been trying to fool him for years, and who sees no benefit in paying more taxes for your services? How do you get this customer to come along with you on this journey?

Your first problem is that you have probably spent a lot of energy for the past twenty or thirty years just keeping those people distant.   It has gotten harder and harder as they have gotten either more passive or more frantic to get in.   You haven't dared to give them an opening by asking what they think because it seems clear that a small group might sack the place, and the majority would stand around and watch. It would be 410 A.D. and the fall of Rome all over again.

So your principals and your superintendents, if they are going to survive, get good at blowing smoke, telling the half-truth; not exactly a lie, but just good news in the best light. This customer, the community, who's certainly not blind, gets more and more mistrustful and alienated, and this atmosphere touches every level, from school and family to state house and legislators.

THE PARENTS' SPECIAL EXPERTISE

Now, suddenly, you have started this thing called restructuring and you need this customer's support. You need them to be well-informed, balanced, broad and willing to take some risks. Not easy given the history mentioned above, but given the new task, it is not achievable without them.

There are at least four clear and compelling reasons for inviting parents and community in, although they tend to get obscured in all the rhetoric about "rights" and "community power." You desperately *need those parents to come inside...as outsiders. You need their expertise...as outsiders.* And, it is important to be very crisp and clear about exactly what kind of expertise parents bring to the process. It is equally *important to distinguish between their expertise and the expertise of the professional educator.* Only then can you begin to listen to each other.

The parent brings two kinds of expertise. The first is as the parent of a particular child. Even if you are the best sixth-grade teacher in the world, you need that expertise. Those parents see a part of that child you don't get to see. They are the ones who hear tears from the upstairs bedroom at 11:00 at night. They are the ones who wander up and murmur, "What's up, babe?" And that is how they find out that the great algebra lesson you taught yesterday didn't work. This student didn't get it. The parent may not know why. He's not qualified to tell you how to teach a better lesson. But, he's got a piece of data that you need and he is the only one who can give it to you.

"...it is important to be very crisp and clear about exactly what kind of expertise parents bring to the process."

There is a second kind of expertise that the parent offers, and that is the expertise of the customer. Let's say Ford has the best truck transmission designer in the world working on staff. She can design those things any way you want. She has thirty years of experience and knows all there is to know about designing truck transmissions. So why would she need to listen to you? You don't know anything about designing transmissions. You don't even know what one looks like. All you do is buy a truck and drive it.

But, if she is any good at all, let alone the best, she wants your data and she wants it all the time in constant feedback. The reason she wants your data is that only you have the expertise of driving that truck under *your* conditions. No matter how good she is as a designer, she has no idea how it feels when you take that truck through creeks while you are hunting quail, or what happens when you pull a horse trailer up the hill on a gravel road. That's why your expertise as a customer is going to be invaluable to her.

The parent of this child in this community brings the same unique expertise to the table. But it is not the expertise of someone who has taught biology for twenty years to seventeen-year-olds, or gotten a generation of six-year-olds launched on a lifetime of reading. To confuse the two kinds of expertise is to confuse the fundamental boundaries, roles and responsibilities.

"To confuse the two kinds of expertise is to confuse the fundamental boundaries, roles and responsibilities."

You need to start with this kind of distinction around differing expertise and different sources of legitimacy or you will end up simply fighting for turf based on power and shrillness. You need somehow to say to the parents, "We want you in here. We need your data. But we don't want you telling that teacher *how* to teach biology.

She has been doing it for thirty years. What she needs to know from you is how its working, how her teaching is affecting your child. Help her with your feedback, but don't tell her what to do in her bailiwick."

MONEY: NOW YOU SEE IT, NOW YOU DON'T

The second reason you need those parents is that they are paying. Twenty years ago, you could count on them as well as the other eighty percent of the community who didn't have children in school, to keep on paying forever. The customer was a given, and had been for so long that you could take them for granted.

The customer is not a given any more, and you no longer have their unquestioned support. Those days are gone and will never be back. Like it or not, you are in the marketplace now, competing for their support in a world of shrinking resources and increasing demands. You can't afford to shut them out.

If you had pulled a group of health care professionals together in 1981 and said, "How is it going, Little Sisters of the Poor?" "How's it going, County Hospital?" "How's it going, Physicians and Nurses?" you would have heard: "Oh things are going pretty well. Costs are rising, we have some problems with quality, people aren't too happy about some of the service, but we're doing it the best way we know how - the way we've always done it."

About ten years later, some half a dozen corporations control nearly forty-percent of the health care business in the U.S., and it just happens that they are for-profit organizations.

One of them acquired a hospital every other day in 1992. If this could happen in health care, why couldn't it happen to public education?

Right now there is a rising chorus of people saying, "Give *us* the money for education and we will build something entirely new; not spend all this time and

"If parents and community are not significantly involved in restructuring they cannot and will not support it, and will, in fact, block any and every real change effort."

money with this old, resistant system. Let us run your high schools on a contract basis. Let the parents have the money and decide where to educate their children." This customer is moving toward these hard questions of quality, cost and choice, and if the system can't learn how to move with him, the customer is gone. You can either see this as a great threat, or a source of energy to move a system. One leads to paralysis and the other to transition.

RULE NUMBER ONE:
BRING THE PARENTS WITH YOU

The third reason you want those parents inside helping you is that *you need their permission*. You can't change anything unless you bring them along with you.

They may have told you in a dozen different ways that they want educational results improved, that they are not satisfied with the way things are. But as soon as something starts to change without their input, they'll start to scream "What are you doing with my kids? Don't change it!" They may not like what they've got now, but it does not follow that they are going to let you touch it.

If parents and community are not significantly involved in restructuring, they cannot and will not support it, and will, in fact, block any and every real change effort. They need to understand what you are up against. What the options are and to help create them. What to expect. You need them to give you permission and to understand what is happening, the same way you need the anchors to give permission and understand what it is they have agreed to. If the parents are with you, they will bring the community with them. If they are not, they will stop you dead. You need their energy to sustain you in the effort. And, most of all, you need their protection when hostile winds blow down on you.

Because this thing we call public education is naked and vulnerable, and increasingly, there are well organized small groups out there who understand that, and they can put a level of fear into the system that is truly terrible. The only thing that can protect you is the community, saying to those people, "These are *our* kids. *Our* schools. *Our* professionals. We trust them. We know what they are doing. They are listening to us. *Back off!*"

**"The more deeply that external group of parents and community
is empowered to participate, the greater the power for change
it can and will generate. But this is true only if the system views
them with respect, sees them as the reason it exists in the first place,
and invites their input, their data and their collaboration."**

Every system, if it's to be an open, learning system, somewhere understands that the customer is the source of great energy precisely because the world and its desires and needs change. The more deeply that external group of parents and community is empowered to participate, the greater the power for change it can and will generate. But this is true only if the system views them with respect, sees them as the reason it exists in the first place, and invites their input, their data and their collaboration. This alliance of mutual respect between school and community is the source of profound learning and growth for both.

MARKETING TO THE COMMUNITY

Without this external voice, in fact, the internal questions of restructuring become moot. No matter what you come up with, its chances for success are slim. So, along with the skills of group process and problem solving and consensual decision making, you will have to acquire yet another expertise. You will have to learn, in a way that is new to public education, how to go out there and bring this customer in. The rest of the world knows how to do this; it is too often alien to educators.

A year ago, just before the holidays, I spent three days with a firm that is a leader in marketing soaps, shampoos, and other personal care products. The specific client was a small product development team in its second year of struggling to launch a new bar of soap. Their tests had not gone well in three sites and they were back to the drawing board with an impressive energy, building their strategy for the third year - new lather, new packaging, new scent - all this for a new bar of soap. They were going to make you and me want that bar of soap.

The following two days found me in a workshop with about one hundred principals in St. Louis. I had just finished talking about how critical the parents and community were when two of them stood up, and in a somewhat whining tone said, "You're telling us we need the parents, but we had two meetings last month, and no one came." And all I could envision at that moment was the product team wrestling with its soap, determined to make us a customer if it took five years.

We don't yet understand the value of the "customer," how much we need the loyalty and their input, and how hard it is to get it. We have to learn how to make a customer of parent and community. It has to be part of a long-term and dedicated strategy, and we are just beginning to think about it seriously. To educate children without a deep partnership of teacher and parent is hopeless, and going in we have conditioned everyone to minimal interaction, indifference, maybe even suspicion. That is the Steady State in most of the country. And, it has to change.

Chapter Fifteen: Some Final Thoughts on Pace, Pain and Gracefulness

The real crisis in restructuring comes just as it starts to happen.   The first year has been spent carefully laying the groundwork, setting it up so that some solid structures are in place against the dysfunctions.   In the second year you start getting better at this stuff, learning how to torque the system enough so that it will move, and yet not shatter into polarities. By the third year, if the work has been done carefully and well, you should be cutting deeply into substantive issues.

Now, the whole thing threatens to come apart. Out there in the "real world" -- the world of state legislatures and school board elections and interest groups -- people want to see results. They want to see improved test scores, and they want them now. They want some dramatic change in comparative rankings, something to show for three years of talk. It is small comfort to the parents of a sixth-grader to hear that by the time that child graduates from high school, her school and her district will be transformed. She can't wait that long. This is the ultimate test of how well you have done your work.

The problem is that we are operating within two kinds of time: "everyday time" and "organizational time." In everyday time, we have cognitive, linear expectations: cause and effect follow one another in some timely, observable, straightforward way. That kind of mindset fits right in with the top-down, command/demand culture of the Western organization. Things like "strategic planning" capture this need to try to control the future.

However, "organizational time" has its own logic. It is non-linear, cumulative, organic, irregular. It doubles back on itself and suddenly moves forward. Anything you make happen overnight tends to get sloughed off, and much of what really occurs is imperceptible in the increments. You can't understand change if you don't understand organizational time.

"You first have to unstick a system, unstick the old roles and attitudes before you can get parents and teachers to begin to experiment, and then to allow the experiment to unfold at the site level."

Entering the third year of a change effort, you can hear the clock ticking. The short-term numbers-driven planning model comes with all the force of its 2000 year history and all the urgency of an educational system in crisis, demanding to see results. And when things don't happen visibly, the top leadership is powerfully tempted to move on to some other solution. In organizational time, it is almost impossible to deliver the kind of measurable improvement you are looking for before the fifth and sixth year. The reason is crystal clear. You first have to unstick a system, unstick the old roles and attitudes before you can get parents and teachers to begin to experiment, and then to allow the experiment to unfold at the site level. That only happens in the third and fourth year, and you won't see results until after that.

Practically, on the district level, this poses a set of tough questions. If you are attempting a long-term change effort, and want to avoid the pilot project syndrome, one solution is to have a phase-in strategy over the first three years, in which you begin with a third of the system the first year, move to two-thirds the second year, and get to a full set of structures by the third year. That allows you to sequence the support staff and resources, and it also allows the larger system to have time in the first year or year-and-a-half to get used to dealing with the flow of bottom-up data, the demands for time, and the shifts in decision-making. When you are talking organizational time, these three years are critical. You cannot load and position the change powerfully enough, too early. The system takes a good long time to test these kinds of strategies, and you have to win back almost two-times the system from cynicism and deep alienation.

"Very often (rankings) are based on infinitesimal statistical differences between and among groups."

By the third and fourth year you should be running hard enough and powerfully enough to unstick a deeply structured system in a significant way. By the fifth and sixth year, you should expect to show significant changes with respect to roles, relationships, and now measurable results as well. The dilemma is to buy enough "real time" for the organizational time to run its course.

You can't spin the scores, but you can spin the process, and therein lies your best hope. If you can engage a significant number of faculty and staff early-on, so that they are involved differently, and the parents understand you are really trying, really listening, it can mitigate the demand for short-term results. If you can do that in the first two to three years, they will stay with you for the long haul, the six or seven years it may take to transform the school.

It's as though you had a lemon of a car and the dealer knew there was nothing he could do to change it. Each time you took it back to him, he'd say, "Oh my, you're back again. I'm terribly sorry. I'll fix this as quickly as possible, and in the meantime, please take this loaner to drive." Chances are, you'd stay with him, and even buy another car from him when you were ready to unload the lemon.

Some of the pressure is imposed from outside. There is a truly pernicious practice, in which schools in a district are ranked one against the other, and the same thing is repeated on the state level. The rankings are then published in a newspaper, and the parents get to read that their school slipped from 15th to 17th in the district rankings, and the district as a whole is not doing nearly as well as some other districts in the state. It effects everything: real estate values, racial politics, educators' careers, students' futures. And the rankings, at least as they are presented, tell nothing. Very often they are based on infinitesimal statistical differences between and among groups.

It doesn't give you any sense of how a school is doing to see that it fell from 15th to 17th place in one year, or that it didn't graduate as many National Merit semi-finalists as the school at the other end of town. The rankings don't tell you what kinds of adults were graduating out of these schools - whether they were able to go out and make the most of the opportunities available to them. They are devoid of any qualitative dimensions.

Every year, the business magazines rank the major MBA programs in the country, and a lot of college seniors probably make decisions on the basis of those rankings. But what Harvard and Stanford and Northwestern do with respect to an MBA is not quantifiable. What's important for a possible student is some descriptive analysis at a qualitative level of how the faculty works, how the students work within that environment, what the experiences are, what they learn about themselves, where they go to work and what they try to do with their education. These are the indicators that truly matter, but as long as those annual rankings in the newspaper are allowed to tell the whole story of a school or a district, the focus will be warped. Again and again, the discussion should return to the values and the qualitative expectations of the community.

Finally, there is the quality I would call "grace." These are ungentle times, and education in particular is an emotional issue. The labor/management/Board relationship at Boundary One is not what it should be. Within the organization, silo to silo are often set against one another. People come into this with a mixture of good will and anxiety, distrust and desire to collaborate. They come as human beings. That means that even after they have committed to a certain direction, or a changed course of behavior, they will not always be able to hold to it. They will fail each other and themselves, because this is difficult behavioral change and it goes against old habits.

"...grace comes from understanding how difficult this business is, and from making the very best assumptions about people and their desire tochange, understanding the reality of past experience and of the culture o often in place."

It may seem strange to end an essay on school restructuring with a comment on personal forgiveness, but that is always where I find myself in the deep and long-term change process. What we need, very often, more than anything else, is a "grace" with one another. This grace comes from understanding how difficult this business is, and from making the very best assumptions about people and their desire to change, understanding the reality of past experience and of the culture so often in place. It is *hard* to make these changes and we will never get it right at the very beginning.

But anyone who watches men and women and children struggle to bring health to their relationships, and improvement to the quality of what they do, cannot help but be impressed with their ability to make deep changes and to succeed. Systems are hard and resistant, but individuals can be their match. It is the giving of "grace" to one another that very often allows us to move through the early sticking moments and gather enough momentum and enough contrary information about one another that we stay the course.

This work we are about is as important a work as there is to be done. We must do it with courage, and with vision, but we must also do it with good theory and deep experience and practice - and some grace.

APPENDIX A:

Examples of Contract Language

EXAMPLE ONE:
AGREEMENT BETWEEN
Two Rivers Public School District
(Board of Education)
and
Two Rivers Education Association (TREA)
Two Rivers, Wisconsin

AGREEMENT TO COLLABORATE

between the

Two Rivers Public School District (Board of Education)
and
Two Rivers Education Association (TREA)

September, 1993 (Rev. 10/93)

SECTION 1 — SITE-BASED DECISION-MAKING

The Two Rivers School Board and the Two Rivers Education Association (TREA) agree to explore a process of decision-making that will deliberately place greater authority and responsibility for education and related decisions within the school itself. The School Board and the TREA will jointly explore changes in structures and procedures that will facilitate this change with the goals of:

- providing better collaboration in quality educational services;
- placing the decision-making closer to the teaching and learning;
- creating an environment that can listen better and respond more quickly to the parents and students' needs; and
- improving the work environment of administrators and teachers which is ultimately the learning environment for children.

The parties also believe that in the process of the implementation of Site-Based Decision-Making, there will be a growing sense of openness of communication, trust, and ultimately an attitude to collaboratively solve problems for the education of pupils in the Two Rivers Public School District.

SECTION 2 — OVERSIGHT COMMITTEE

To oversee this process, and guarantee the integrity of this change to Site-Based Decision-Making, an Oversight Committee (Village Partnership Team) shall be formed.

a. It will be made up of:

    Representatives of the TREA (5)
    Administrators (2)
    School Board Member (1)
    Support Staff (1)
    Parents (2)
    Representative of the Community at Large (1)

b. The role of this Oversight Committee will be:

- to give direction and guidelines to the process;
- to make decisions with respect to pace and scope of the process;
- to attain resources and other support for those involved in the form of training sessions and facilitated meetings;

- to establish general steps for preparation and training in the initiating sites;
- to insure that the pace and support are in harmony to provide high quality while keeping the change process moving;
- to collaborate in "unsticking" the process when it runs into difficulties and obstacles; and
- to jointly listen, learn from, and practice themselves the problem-solving at the system level that the school sites will be modeling.

SECTION 3 — SITE COUNCILS

Each school will have a similarly structured committee with representation such that the professional staff (principal and instructional staff) together make-up a simple majority. It should also include parents, other support staff, and in the case of senior high school, student(s) as well. The composition of the Site Councils is subject to the approval of the Oversight Committee. Examples are:

Elementary	Middle School	High School
Building Principal (1)	Building Principal (1)	Building Principal (1)
Classroom Teachers (3)	Classroom Teachers (4)	Classroom Teachers (4 or 5)
Other Instructional Staff/Specials (1)	Other Instructional Staff/Specials (2)	Other Instructional Staff/Specials (2)
Support Staff (1)	Support Staff (1)	Support Staff (2)
Parents (3)	Parents (4)	Parents (4)
Board Member (1) - Ex officio	Board Member (1) - Ex officio	Students (2)
		Board Member (1) - Ex officio
Total Members - 10	Total Members - 13	Total Members - 16 or 17

(The size of the school, the size and complexity of its instructional staff, and its grade levels will all influence the committee composition.)

The Site Council's goal is to make decisions about school issues such as budget, curriculum, staffing, and day-to-day operations of the school. In general, the site council wants to make certain that high quality decisions, that are appropriate, are made at the school level.

(NOTE: No staff member shall be excluded from the bargaining unit as a supervisory managerial employee within the meaning of the Labor Relations Act by reason of his/her participation in Site-Based Management.)

SECTION 4 — LIMITATIONS

The parties agree that we are willing to explore all the implications of the Site-Based Decision-Making process. However, none of us is able to set aside our legal responsibilities or certain dimensions of our organizational roles. Therefore, it is understood that unless exceptions are made, (see Section 5 below) this process cannot change:

- a. State and Federal laws as they pertain to us;
- b. Wisconsin Department of Public Instruction rules and regulations;
- c. Two Rivers School Board policies and administrative regulations; or
- d. the collective bargaining agreements between any of the organized labor groups and the Two Rivers Public School Board.

SECTION 5 — WAIVERS

The Oversight Committee will accept requests for waivers from an existing policy, regulation, or a portion of the labor agreement. These requests will then be referred to the appropriate

98   mechanism for action (i.e. take to TREA if issue deals with the Master Agreement, take to Board
99   of Education if issue deals with Board Policy, etc.)

101   a.   It is clearly understood that these exceptions, are not precedent setting, not system-
102   wide.
103   b.   The exceptions are temporary and are automatically rescinded each June 15 unless
104   specifically extended.
105   c.   The sites report to the Oversight Committee the implications, successes and failures
106   based on these exceptions.

108 SECTION 6 — VOLUNTARY INVOLVEMENT

110   Involvement in this process, at least in its first steps, is voluntary on the part of individuals and
111   school sites. Schools will not be forced early on into this Site-Based Decision-Making process.

113   Individuals within schools also are free not to participate even if one's school is chosen.
114   Obviously, the Oversight Committee hopes there will be a strong majority in participating
115   schools to insure the environments in these schools will be very participative, team oriented, and
116   parent and child focused.

118   At the same time, no adverse employment action will be taken against any staff member because
119   of his/her non-participation in a Site-Based Decision-Making arrangement.

121 SECTION 7 — SLOWING OR WITHDRAWAL.

123   The parties recognize that the mutual exploration of Site-Based Decision-Making may lead into
124   difficult areas and unforeseen problems. We each take this risk in good faith and with a
125   readiness to examine our own attitudes and behaviors and improve together. So that each side
126   may have the necessary safeguards and acceptance of the process, the School Board or the TREA
127   has the right to request either a slowdown and, in extreme cases, a withdrawal from the joint
128   process.

130   Each side can exercise this option by a formal letter to the other stating the desire to slow down
131   or withdraw, and state the reasons. There will then be a "cooling off" period of 60 days during
132   which the sides will meet at least twice to discuss the issue(s), possibly using a third party
133   consultant. If after the 60 day period one party wants to withdraw, the process and agreement
134   will be considered terminated.

137   The terms of this collaborative agreement have been accepted and approved by the afore
138   mentioned parties as witnessed below.

141   _Patrick K Hagnon_   _10/25/93_
142   President, Two Rivers Board of Education   Date

145   _Robert Burns_   _10/26/93_
146   President, Two Rivers Education Association   Date

149   _Scott Mack_   _10/26/93_
150   District Administrator   Date

EXAMPLE TWO:
AGREEMENT BETWEEN
Eugene School District 4J
and
Eugene Education Association (EEA)
Eugene, Oregon

ARTICLE XVIII - CLASS SIZE

The District and the Association recognize class size as a critical component of the District's ability to achieve its educational mission, students' opportunity to learn, and each teacher's ability to be an effective educator. The parties agree that a mutual effort must continue to be made to study and where necessary reduce class size. The Joint Class Size Committee shall continue.

The charge, duties, responsibilities and expectations of the Committee will be found in Appendix D.

ARTICLE XIX - SITE BASED DECISION MAKING

SITE-BASED DECISION MAKING (SBDM): The District and the Association believe that Site-Based Decision Making, a governance model in which Unit Members (teachers) and other stakeholders are given increased responsibility for making decisions with regard to their day-to-day affairs, has the potential to improve education, foster mutual respect, provide greater employee empowerment, improve the quality and extent of parent involvement, create an environment which is more responsible to the client needs and concerns, and encourage the collegial exchange of ideas. To this end, the parties pledge themselves to an honest and mutual examination and trial of site-based decision making.

19.1   THE DISTRICT SITE-BASED STEERING COMMITTEE (Steering Committee): This collaborative Committee shall be established for the purpose of helping guide and assist District staff with SBDM and shall be composed of the following:
- Six (6) Unit Members (Teachers) (May include the Association President)
- Three (3) Administrators
- Four (4) Parents
- Two (2) Classified Persons
- The Superintendent
- The OSEA Consultant and President (if not included above) as ex-officio
- The EEA Consultant and President (if not included above) as ex-officio
- The Human Resources Director as ex-officio
- One (1) School Board Member as ex-officio

a.   District Site-Based Steering Committee Responsibilities: The Steering Committee will perform these major functions:

1. Provide leadership and set direction for the implementation and management of SBDM. The Steering Committee will use the SBDM Study Committee's Report and Recommendations as its foundation.

2. Develop SBDM procedural guidelines and make them available to all District personnel.

3. Develop a SBDM training program.

4. Recommend sites for participation in SBDM.

5. Establish procedures for responding to individual site questions and concerns regarding SBDM.

6. Identify funds needed for SBDM and allocate SBDM funds to approved sites.

b. Work site or school site committee: The work or school site committee shall consist of at least the following:

1. A majority of school site committee members shall be unit members. Membership shall be voluntary. Unit members will be elected by unit members.

2. Each school site committee shall include the following stakeholders: Unit members, administrators, classified employees, and parents.

3. Each stakeholder group has a right to veto committee proposals. Work sites may request assistance from the Steering Committee to resolve issues.

19.2 BOUNDARIES OR PARAMETERS OF SBDM: Recognizing legal responsibilities, the parties agree that unless mutually agreed exceptions are made, they will adhere to:

a. State and Federal Laws and Regulations

b. District School Board Policies and District Regulations

c. Collective Bargaining Agreements and memorandums between the District and its employee groups.

19.3 VOLUNTARY NATURE: The parties agree to limit the scope
      of SBDM during this trial period of learning and exploration
      to:

      a.   Site Participation.

           1.   Sites selected for participation from those that
                volunteer.

           2.   Appropriate training will be required for each
                selected site.

      b.   Individual Participation.

           1.   Unit members will participate on SBDM committees
                and in leadership roles on a voluntary basis.

           2.   Unit members who choose not to participate in SBDM
                leadership or committee responsibilities will not
                be adversely evaluated.

           3.   However, all staff at a SBDM site are responsible
                for implementing site decisions.

19.4 IMPLEMENTATION: The District agrees to budget funds for
      SBDM training, compensation, and implementation.

      a.   Local sites approved for SBDM will be allocated funds by
           the Steering Committee for that purpose. Compensation,
           for Association members who assume leadership positions
           at the local site, shall be consistent with the terms of
           the contract.

      b.   Compensation may take the form of:

           1.   Release time
           2.   Additional salary
           3.   Extended contract
           4.   Reduced assignment schedule
           5.   Or other mutually agreeable forms of compensation

      c.   Site Compensation/Training plans will be reviewed and
           approved by the Steering Committee.

19.5 WAIVERS:

      The District and the Association each recognize that all
      legal contractual rights and obligations remain in full force
      and effect unless either party waives the right or
      obligation.

A request for waiver by a site shall be sent to the Steering Committee for consideration. They will forward to the District and the Association only those recommendations which the committee supports.

The Steering Committee may recommend to District/Association that individual sites be given a waiver from a provision of existing policy, regulation, District practice, or a labor agreement.

19.6   The funds necessary to implement SBDM will be allocated from*p240X

19.7   SAFETY NET CLAUSE: The parties recognize that our mutual exploration of SBDM may result in unforeseen difficulties or problem areas. Since our initial foray into SBDM is largely experimental, we agree that either party may want to slow down or halt, at least temporarily, the movement toward SBDM. The safety net process is established for this purpose.

To initiate the safety net process, the Association or District must send the other a letter stating the concerns and reasons for instituting the safety net. The parties shall then have thirty (30) days to resolve the initiating parties' concerns. If the concerns are not resolved after thirty (30) days, then all plans for extending approval for the addition of sites to SBDM shall be placed on "hold" until the parties reach agreement on how to proceed. The parties agree to use a mutually acceptable facilitator to bring resolution.

In witness whereof, the Association has caused this Agreement to be signed by its President and attested to by its Secretary and the Board has caused this Agreement to be signed by its Chairperson, attested by its Clerk.

EUGENE EDUCATION ASSOCIATION

EUGENE SCHOOL DISTRICT No. 4J
LANE COUNTY, OREGON

By: _____

By: _____

ATTEST: _____

ATTEST: _____

By: _____

By: _____

Date 5/6/93

Date 5/10/93

EXAMPLE THREE:
AGREEMENT BETWEEN
Everett School District
and
Everett Education Association/
United Teachers of Everett
Everett, Washington

MEMORANDUM OF UNDERSTANDING AND AGREEMENT
SITE-BASED DECISION MAKING

The Everett School District and the Everett Education Association/United Teachers of Everett agree that shared decision making should be fostered and promoted in accordance with the provisions contained herein.

1. The District and Association believe that arrangements which provide an increased role for employees to make decisions on matters that affect them can foster the exchange of ideas and information that is necessary to improve education for students and to increase employee job performance, satisfaction and morale.

    The District and Association agree that better decisions will be made and should be fostered through shared decision making procedures at all sites in the District. To this end, the District and Association will promote and assist employees in the development of shared decision making processes and procedures across the District.

2. In support of these goals, the parties agree that the Superintendent, Association President and any additional representatives designated by the District and Association respectively, shall periodically meet during 1993-94 for the following purposes.

    a. Facilitate the implementation of the Everett School District Site-Based Decision Making model through this and other agreements between the District and Association regarding shared decision making. This would include seeking waivers of the Collective Bargaining Agreement where deemed appropriate by both parties through processes established by each party.

    b. Ensure that Site-Based Decision Making activities do not interfere with employee preparation periods as provided for by the Collective Bargaining Agreement, unless the Association and District agree otherwise.

    c. Assess the impact of Site-Based Decision Making activities on the use of time and its impact on job responsibilities.

    d. Provide necessary resources and ensure that reasonable financial resources are made available to each site as the staff prepares for and implements Site-Based Decision Making procedures and plans.

e.   Advise and assist, as needed, District regional teams and schools in the development of their procedures, processes and structures for shared decision making.

3.   Concerns of either party relating to shared decision making beyond the 1993-94 school year will be considered appropriate subjects for further examination by the parties during successor agreement negotiations.

4.   Either party may, at any point, notify the other of its intent to withdraw from this Memorandum of Understanding and Agreement. Said party will provide written notification to the other of its intent, allowing a sixty day waiting period. During this waiting period, the District and Association representatives will come together to attempt to identify and resolve differences.

5.   This Memorandum of Understanding and Agreement will be effective upon its ratification by each party through established processes.

x _____   _____
For the District   For the Association

Date ___11/8/93___   Date ___11/22/93___

x _____
For the Board of Directors,
Everett School District

Date ___11/8/93___

APPENDIX B:

Mission and Goals

- ■Beliefs Statement
- ■School District Mission
- ■Planning Assumptions
- ■Goals
- ■Strategic Plan

as developed by
Two Rivers Public School District
Two Rivers, Wisconsin

179

TWO RIVERS PUBLIC SCHOOLS
THE STRATEGIC PLAN

These are highlights of the actual strategic plan. There is additional detail in the original document.

1.   By the year 2000 all children will start school ready to learn.

2.   By the year 2000, the high school graduation rate will increase to at least 90 percent.

3.   By the year 2000, students will leave grades four, eight, and twelve having demonstrated competency in challenging subject matter including English, mathematics, science, history, and geography; and every school will ensure that all students learn to use their minds well, so they may be prepared for responsible citizenship, further learning, and productive employment in our modern economy.

4.   By the year 2000, American students will be first in the world in science and mathematics achievement.

5.   By the year 2000, every adult will be literate and will possess the knowledge and skills necessary to compete in a global economy and exercise the rights and responsibilities of citizenship.

6.   By the year 2000, every school in America will be free of drugs and violence and will offer a disciplined environment conducive to learning.

PLANNING ASSUMPTIONS

1.   There will be no significant changes in the community employment and economic picture that will have an effect on the projected enrollments.

2.   All students in the Two Rivers Public School District should have access to reasonably equal educational facilities and opportunities.

3.   The students and graduates are a part of a global society composed of individuals from different cultures who speak different languages, have varying religious beliefs, and who embrace a wide range of political views.

4.   The School District's educational offerings and services should be a reflection of the staff and community.

5.   State mandated items would be funded by the state or implementation would be done at the District's discretion.

6.   The "state" will fund the educational programs at a realistic level (not less than 1990-91).

STATEMENT OF BELIEFS

The Two Rivers Public School District believes that all students can learn and that the District has a responsibility to provide educational opportunities to all as students. We believe that students should graduate equipped with specific academic skills and a motivation for life-long learning. It is our belief that education provides the best possible avenue for students to achieve satisfying lives and to be productive members of an interdependent global society.

We believe the educational program of this District must reflect community needs and receive support form the total community to be an exemplary educational system.

SCHOOL DISTRICT MISSION

The Two Rivers Public School District shall assist each student, commensurate with his/her abilities, to achieve the following:

A.   Development of pride and motivation in personal effort and achievement.

B.   Competence in analytical thinking, problem-solving, decision making, and creativity.

C.   Development of a value system that promotes successful human relationships, including family and parenting skills, that promotes personal responsibility, encourages social ethics, citizenship and sensitivity to community responsibility, and that enhances the student's ability to function cooperatively in society.

D.   Competence in the basic skills: reading, writing, communication (speaking and listening), and mathematics.

E.   Preparation for post-secondary school experiences including the "world of work," further formal education, direct education for employment, and appreciation of life-long learning.

F.   Understanding and appreciation of the fine arts, humanities, natural sciences, social sciences, and developing technology.

G.   Understanding and application of principles which contribute to a heathy body and mind.

APPENDIX C:

A State Model of Systemic Change -

The Village Partnership in Wisconsin

Included here is a brief summary of the first two years of a systemic approach to restructuring of public schools in Wisconsin. If the state is the educational system in the United States, then we must take into account those elements of the Steady State that hold it in place from within (unions, school boards, administrators), and to some extent from without (parents, business community, legislators).

The Wisconsin Teachers Union, Wisconsin Education Association (WEAC), and its arch rival the Wisconsin Manufacturers and Commerce (WMC) have been doing battle throughout the 1980's with some mutual damage but surely no results for public education.

These groups came together in Wausau, Wisconsin, in March of 1992, and invited other major actors such as the American Federation of Teachers (AFT), the Wisconsin Association of School Boards (WASB), representatives of the Superintendents and Principals Associations for the State (WASDA), and a separate group of management and labor from Milwaukee (MTEA). Tom Paysant, Superintendent of San Diego at the time, talked about collaboration and decentralization in San Diego.

Out of that meeting came a preliminary agreement signed by the eight attendant groups to try some other approach to school improvement and restructuring in Wisconsin based on a collaborative approach.

The number of organizations involved grew from eight to twelve, formed a not-for-profit corporation, and began to seek funds "to promote systemic, statewide major reform in Wisconsin schools." They received an initial grant from the Aid Association for Lutherans (AAL), for $225,000, and were joined by other private sector supports throughout 1993.

Twenty-two school districts requested membership in the first workshop of The Village Partnership as the new structure was called. The goal was to elevate the systemic learning strategy outlined in this monograph to several other levels, including a learning network of the schools and, of course, the state structure made up of:

Association of Wisconsin School Administrators (AWSA)

Cooperative Educational Service Agencies (CESA)

Milwaukee Public Schools (MPS)

Milwaukee Teachers Education Association (MTEA)

University of Wisconsin System (UWS)

Wisconsin Association of School Boards (WASB)

Wisconsin Association of School District Administrators (WASDA)

Wisconsin Congress of Parents and Teachers (WPTA)

Wisconsin Department of Public Instruction (WDPI)

Wisconsin Education Association Council (WEAC)

Wisconsin Federation of Teachers (WFT)

Wisconsin Manufacturers and Commerce (WMC)

Wisconsin Technical College System (WTCS)

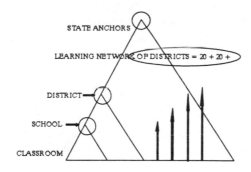

It should be viewed as a parallel structure now that leads from classroom and school site, to district board, union and management leaders, to a *network of districts*, to the state anchors.

185

The first network of district oversite teams met on February 23-26, 1993. They met a second time October 11-12, 1993, to share their learning and deepen their exposure to theories of change. Regional orientation meetings were held throughout the state in November and December of 1993. More than a thousand people attended these one-day seminars.

A second wave of districts was chosen in November of 1993 and began work in February, 1994. Each learning network is scheduled to meet twice a year to deepen its learning and share its experience, as well as begin to shape ideas for change at the state level among the anchors that would further enable their restructuring and responsiveness at the site.

Movement is slow, but the alternative of every district for itself again, flies in the face of systemic change much the way the pilot school does. The cumulative power of many districts learning and moving together creates at least the possibility of a counter strong enough to be heard and reckoned with.

Finally, the change that is already apparent is one of linkage, respect, and understanding at the state level among organizations that have little if any official ties and usually speak to each other only shrilly through the media.

Minnesota has begun a similar statewide strategy as of this writing, has launched its first fifteen districts, and is seeking both private and public funding for the next five years. Similar networks are emerging in the state of Washington, driven by the NEA locals and their councils in the east and west sections of the state. The same is true of Nebraska.

APPENDIX D:
Example
Diagnosis of a
School District

Eugene School District 4J
Eugene, Oregon

The following is an excerpt from the diagnostic report assembled by the Eugene, Oregon Public Schools Oversite Committee. This is an example of a district listening to the system's boundaries and roles at the beginning of a restructuring process.

DIAGNOSTIC FINDINGS AND CONCLUSIONS

INTRODUCTION

The study committee wanted to determine the current status of the district, its general readiness for change, and the issues that were important to consider if the district decided to implement site-based decision making. Early in its deliberations, several questions were identified:

Would a change to site-based decision making be too painful?

Would the change be too negative?

Would the implementation of site-based decision making set the district back?

Is the district too complacent?

Committee members devised an interview form and process to allow them to listen to what district employees, members of the community, parents, students, and school board members had to say about the school district. About 200 people were interviewed. Specifically, people were asked about the relationship between labor and management, the role of teachers and support staff, the role of the principal, the flow of information, the role of the central administration, and the perception of parents and the community.

FINDINGS

School District 4J is a complex and richly textured organization. There are many options for students and parents, and there are many diverse and sometimes contradictory opinions and beliefs about the school district. It is only when one begins to understand how these contradictory perceptions fit together that one begins to understand the system as a whole.

While it is a diverse and complex system, and while there are contradictory opinions about almost everything, several common themes were identified. There are issues and problems, but staff, parents, and the community generally are positive about the school district. They feel good about sending their children to school and they feel good about working here. Both the staff and the community have high expectations of 4J. Staff and parents are tremendously dedicated to the education of their children and expect that the quality of education will be excellent. At the same time, there is the expectation that there be no failure. One person being interviewed said, "you are expected to be creative, but you better not fail."

GENERAL THEMES

"Compared with other organizations there is respect and an uncommon willingness to work through issues without confrontation. This is recent and very positive."

There is a growing sense of collaboration within the district. Recent collaborative bargaining initiatives are making a difference, but there is concern that "the formalization of the labor and management designations still inhibits the process of working together as one toward one goal."

188

"I don't understand what you do, so therefore, it's not important."

This school district is decentralized and the staff and parents are able to operate so independently that there is frequent misunderstanding about what others in the district do. Staff and parents are, more often than not, pleased with their school, or their department, or their teacher, but they do not understand and are suspicious about what other schools, other teachers, and other departments do. There is a lack of understanding about the work of the Education Center and a major difference between what those who work there believe about it and what those who have little contact with it believe.

"Respect, the need for it and the lack of it."

People work hard and perform well, but believe they are unrecognized for the jobs they do and for the stress involved in doing those jobs. Some teachers believe they are not respected by the community; parents, especially minority parents, believe they are not respected by teachers; and those who work at the Education Center believe they are not respected by the rest of the system. Teachers believe they are not respected by students, and classified employees feel under-valued by teachers. Principals are caught in-between.

Motives are questioned. For example, some teachers fear that a move to site-based decision making means that parents will try to become too involved in making decisions about curriculum and teaching techniques or that, as teachers, they will be asked to make the unpleasant decisions others don't want to make. Some parents and teachers fear that the administration is giving "lip service" to wanting to increase parent and staff involvement but really intends to maintain control.

"Busy--moving in many directions: rewarding, exciting, distracting, and frustrating."

Employees like working in 4J. They have high expectations for themselves and for each other. They report that problems of the past are being worked on, but they fear that they will have increased workloads and less time and fewer resources to do their jobs. They are bothered by the increased negative political focus on public education, worried about how they are going to meet the increased demands, and concerned about the changing population of students who have more needs and more problems then ever before. Employees want to work more with other employees as team members.

"Schools have a level of autonomy that allows for principals and staff to create schools that are significantly different."

School autonomy is the keynote of this school district. It is its key strength and its major weakness. Working and learning conditions at individual sites are not consistent across the district. Some employees and parents are confused and concerned about this diversity, while others feel empowered by it. Some people believe that diversity among schools leads to unequal opportunities for students. Many individuals (staff and parents, and the community) identify with their site rather than with the district. Teachers and principals have a great deal of autonomy and feel empowered to do their jobs. Individual sites have cohesiveness but do not feel connected to the district or to other schools or departments.

189

THE CURRENT STATE OF THE SIX SPECIFIC ROLES

Role 1: _The Labor/Management Relationship._ **"Getting better, but guarded."**

While the relationship and the way negotiations are being done is improving, there continue to be comments that the unions don't represent the individual, that the relationship is adversarial, that the contract limits the ability of teachers to be professional, and that the relationship is controlling, both of the workers and of the administrators. Many people see the labor-management relationship as being very site-specific: "within our own building there is a close working relationship. There are problems in other parts of the district." Classified workers generally do not feel as good about the relationship as do teachers.

Role 2: _Role of Teachers, Support Staff, and Students_

Teachers. **"I always thought I wanted to be a teacher until I worked in the schools. I would not want to be a teacher. They are underpaid and over-worked. The community doesn't understand what they do."**

People view the teaching staff as a group deeply dedicated to their vocation, excited and caring about children. At the same time they are stressed, competitive, and quite often at odds with the growing complexity and demands of the role, and increasingly under attack from people and groups that have no relationship or contact with the school at all. They would like more staff development. One teacher said, "we are expected to wear many hats and solve many social problems. I wasn't trained for all this, but I feel guilty for being inadequate."

Classified. **"They walk behind but would rather walk alongside:"**

The one employee group that expresses significant dissatisfaction is the classified workers, particularly those working in the Facilities Management Department. They are dissatisfied with the last round of negotiations and see themselves as being "second-class citizens" who get the "leftovers in pay and benefits." They represent a diverse group of interests which makes it hard to get the unity that teachers have. There are secretaries, instructional assistants, cooks, carpenters, plumbers, bus drivers, and electronic technicians. Some are building based and some never visit a school. They believe they are not actively invited to participate in the decision-making process. Some classified workers have worked out a good working relationship and feel empowered by the district, but generally they do not see themselves as, and are not viewed as, an integral part of the educational system.

Students/Learning. **"We are expected to save the world´ and yet we are in a system criticized as `no good.´ No one understands the pressures on us."**

High school students report that there are enormous pressures to succeed in 4J. They express confusion when they read constantly about how poor the quality of education is in the United States.

There is the belief throughout the community that each student has a right to a quality education. However, 4J is viewed as being a "white-collar" district in which only the needs of the academically able are being adequately met. There is staff and community concern that the needs of "at-risk," the non-college bound, and minority students are not being met, and concerns about the lack of a comprehensive vocational and technical education program.

190

-9-

Role 3: _The Role of the Principal._ **"Like the mayor of a small town, whose role is to keep everyone happy."**

Principals are valued and believed to be enormously powerful. They determine the tone of the school, the involvement of parents, the dissemination of information, and figure greatly in the labor/management relationship. Principals are described as being "caught in-between" the Education Center, teachers, and parents. They are seen as being instrumental to the change process. "The principal as site-based implementer is very important, even critical to the model's success."

Those principals who are readily accessible, share power, build coalitions, and are responsive to parents, teachers, support staff, and students are trusted and valued enormously. Those that do not have these attributes are seen as being non-responsive and controlling.

Role 4: _Information System._ **"Information is there..."**

Information is highly valued. Some say there is a surplus of readily available information while others report that it is subject to "bottlenecks or that it is non-existent." Open-Line, the district mail system, and the computer system are viewed as effective and necessary, but there is still dependence on rumor and concern that information "goes in, but does not come out." Some say they must be aggressive to get information and that parents' ability to access it is related to their socioeconomic status.

Role 5: _Education Center._ **"What is their role - leader or servant?"**

There is a lack of understanding about the Education Center and a discrepancy between what those who work there believe about its function and effectiveness and what those who have little contact with it believe.

The individuals at the Education Center are passionate about their work and believe their job is to be responsive to the needs of schools. For some special interest groups (e.g., parents of minority children or parents of children with disabilities) and for certain work groups within the school district (e.g., curriculum, transportation, food services, and maintenance) the knowledge and control from the Education Center is very important. Parents, unless they have children with special interests or needs, report that they "haven't a clue about what goes on" at the Education Center.

Some school staffs, on the other hand, have the opinion that the Education Center is more meddlesome than helpful, and report that it makes decisions without involving them or with which they do not agree. They question the motives of the Education Center and fear that it blocks their freedom to be creative and independent. There are some schools, however, that would like to see the Education Center be directive and controlling.

When talking specifically about what the individual employees in the Education Center do, people understand the need to have central services, value the work of individuals there, and believe them to be supportive of teachers, parents, and groups with special needs. Some even fear the loss of this support.

191

Role 6: Parents and the Community. "**Depends on who you ask.**"

Parents continually strive to make their presence felt, whether in a positive or negative fashion, and have high expectations of the district. Parents share the concern for the quality of education and want the district to meet the needs of all students. They want to be involved in the schools, and they want to help with the decision-making process. Those who are involved with their schools and with the district tend to have more information and receive better service. Those who are not involved are less satisfied. Many are disenfranchised. Parents of elementary-aged students find it easier to be involved. Parents of middle and high school students, students with special needs, and minority students do not express as high a level of satisfaction with the district as other parents; they believe that the district can and should be doing more. As students get into middle and high school, communication, information, and staff encouragement for involvement in decision making decreases.

There are widely differing opinions about the image of the district in the community. Employees say "the community doesn't know us; they know what they read in the newspaper and hear from others." Others say the community does not value children. Some citizens believe that public employees are always at the "public trough." Many citizens value education highly and the community is supportive when there is an identified need.

SPECIFIC ISSUES

As the interviews were conducted, three specific issues were identified. They were not themes and did not arise in a high number of interviews, but they need to be considered.

Minorities: There is a growing awareness of the increasing racial diversity of the school district and concern about racism in the schools. Some minority staff, students, and parents feel that they are treated differently. They want the administration to deal quickly, authoritatively, and centrally with their concerns.

Maintenance: The staff of the Facilities Management Department expressed unhappiness and frustration about their organization and about how they are perceived in the school district. They feel misunderstood and blocked and that their specialized knowledge is not respected.

Change: Those who work within centralized services (e.g., food services, transportation, maintenance, media services) fear that moving to site-based decision making will mean their service is no longer needed or that they will lose control of how their work is done. They worry about their jobs and the effects site-based decision making will have on the school district. Some fear, for example, that a move to site-based decision making could mean decentralized purchasing and therefore an increase in the cost.

192

CONCLUSIONS

This is a richly complex system. There is diversity of thought and opinion and diversity of programs and schools. There is no single "right perception" and there are certainly contradictions, but generally the district is viewed positively by the staff and by the community. There are problems and issues that must be dealt with by the district.

If the district decides to proceed, the information gathered by the committee will help it design implementation strategies and know where it must focus. People have questions and concerns about site-based decision making. They are not actively campaigning against it.

At the outset, committee members posed several questions to be answered before deciding whether or not to recommend that site-based decision making be formally established in 4J. The questions and our answers follow:

Would a change to site-based decision making be too painful? No, but change is difficult and demanding. There are a few schools in 4J that would resist being given more authority. The role of the Education Center would be under extreme scrutiny. Schools and staffs would feel pressure from all sides. But teachers, administrators, and parents already feel that they are empowered and can affect change at their buildings and across the district. Classified staff want to be involved and want to make this a better place for children and a better place to work for themselves. The district has grown, and the staff wants to continue to grow in their ability to work collaboratively.

Would the change be too negative? No. Improved instruction for all students is positive. If those closest to the instructional program should be empowered to design instructional improvements, it would be positive. If the collaborative involvement of students, teachers, the unions, parents, administrators, and the school board in the educational process will help to better govern the district and to make instruction better, it would be positive.

Would the implementation of site-based decision making set the district back? No, there is a need and a desire to improve instruction for all students. There is a desire to improve collaborative working relationships. There is a vagueness about what each other does that needs to be clarified. The boundaries and the rules that are now vague or interpreted differently, or ignored, could be clarified. A process for waiving the rules and boundaries that we find frustrating could be created. The district would only move forward if these desires are met.

Is the district too complacent? No, staff and parents see the need to change and be responsive. They are concerned about the lack of services for students and are critical of themselves and of each another. They care enormously and want to see improvements in the instructional program.

193

-12-

Helpful Contacts Working In Restructuring Efforts

Wisconsin:

Jim Morgan
Project Coordinator
Village Partnership
608-258-3400

Minnesota:

Dawn S. Cole
Project Coordinator
Shared Decisions Minnesota
612-292-4815

Nebraska:

Sue Fulleton
Director
Instructional Advocacy
Nebraska State Education Association (NSEA)
Nebraska Partnership for Educational Progress
402-475-7611

Washington:

Jim Russell
Uniserve Representative
Olympic Uniserve Council
206-779-4818

Dick Iverson
Regional Manager
Washington Education Association
509-326-4046

Iowa:

Gerry Ott
Exeuctive Director
New Iowa Schools Development Corporation (NISDC)
515-226-9852

Helping Countries Working
In Restructuring Efforts